MW00800397

Thanks for your support Dr. Pia Scott (handwritten inscription)

How I Got Over

The Educational Pursuit
of Black Female Scholars

Dr. Pia L. Scott

Copyright 2019 © Dr. Pia L. Scott

All rights reserved. No part of this publication may be reproduced or distributed in any form or by any means, electronic or mechanical, including photocopying, recording, or by any information storage or retrieval system, without the prior written consent of the authors.

ISBN: 978-1-7329895-4-2

Dedication

This book is dedicated in memory of my grandmother Geneva W. Smalls- A women of great wisdom, insight, and love.

Acknowledgments

I would like to acknowledge and thank my mother, Ulanda S. Scott, who is always there for me. I would like to acknowledge Drs. Joyce Pittman and Florence Ferguson for their confidence, humor, and loving support. To all the ancestors and doctors who have paved the way and on whose shoulders we stand.

Foreword

It was once illegal for black people to engage in activity that involved learning to read and write. The quest for knowledge in the black community has always been a priority. Many of our ancestors did not allow the fear of harm or death to stop this pursuit.

Formal education plays a key role for many. Education allows us to gain different perspectives and insights. We are able to make interpretation and provide analysis on various subjects because of gained knowledge.

The authors of *How I Got Over The Educational Pursuit of Black Female Scholars* documents the journey of twelve highly educated black females who pushed passed obstacles, challenges, and many barriers in pursuit of more knowledge. In their educational pursuit, some authors were faced with sickness and in a few instances, death of a loved one. They persevered. Perseverance is the unwritten theme of this collaboration.

These twelve black female scholars earned doctoral degrees in medicine, psychology, education, social work in policy, and pharmacy. As a black female scholar who was also in pursuit of education, I experienced first-hand the struggle that exists in the midst of your pursuit. Life happens, and it happened to me while in my first doctoral program. YES, the first doctoral program, which I did not receive the doctoral degree. Like the authors, I would not be defeated. I had to Act, Assess, and Adjust, and adjust I did.

I successfully defended my dissertation, April 24, 2017, at Howard University in the School of Education. My mantra is #keepgrinding and my message is "Delayed is Not Denied". The stories in *How I Got Over The Educational Pursuit of Black Female Scholars* exemplifies both. The stories are impactful and inspirational and will leave you wanting more.

The authors share exactly how they got over. Those of you who have pursued advanced degrees will begin reflecting on how you were able to reach your goal of attaining that degree. Those of you who are in middle of your educational pursuit, will be motivated to see it to the finish line. If you aspire to take the leap to earn an advanced degree, this book will give you the inspiration you need to begin the process.

Dr. Pia L. Scott and contributing authors have shared vulnerable moments with truth and grace. The power in this anthology is its transparency.

Sharon H. Porter, Ed.D.
Educator. Author. Talk Show Host.
www.sharonhporter.com

Table of Contents

Dr. Pia L. Scott

When I dare to be powerful-to use my strength in the service of my vision, then it becomes less and less important whether I am afraid. —Audre Lorde

There is Power in Purpose
By: Dr. Pia L. Scott, EdD, LPCA, GCDF

Introduction

Growing up in a two-parent household in a middle-class neighborhood, I was the eldest of two children. I grew up in a small town located twenty minutes outside of Charleston, South Carolina. During my school years I dealt with loss, depression, death, self-esteem issues, and other things that just make one want to give up on life. After losing my father at age 11, I thought life was over, but little did I know that my purpose was just beginning. I always knew that my purpose was to serve, especially when it comes to the youth. When you know your purpose, you are more confident and motivated to walk in that purpose. I dare to be powerful, and I become less and less afraid of what I am meant to do in this lifetime. I wish to inspire not just women pursuing their doctorates, but also those that are hoping for change. So much can happen to a person as she goes through things in life.

People often stifle their own growth because they are too busy being concerned with things that do not concern them. Opposition lurks at every corner, but our experiences give us the strength to master each test along the way. Then we come to realize that even in our toughest moments, these trials are meant to bring us closer to our purpose. My purpose led to my pursuit of a doctoral degree. In 2016, I received my doctorate in Educational Leadership and Management with a focus in Higher Education from Drexel University in Philadelphia, Pennsylvania. My background consists of career and professional development, entrepreneurship, and change management. I am inspired to motivate others by sharing my story.

Personal Experiences: Role Models are Important to an Educational Journey

Personal experiences can shape our perceptions. We all face challenges in life, but the way we handle those challenges can ultimately cause us to sink or swim. Some people are blessed to know what their purpose is, and some are still searching for the answer. Others only pursue things for specific reasons such as accolades or the title of "doctor" behind their name. Intentions are not always genuine and having a passion for your purpose is not just something that you declare; it just comes to you naturally. My pursuit was more than just a title, but a passion to make changes in my community. I was intentional about my pursuit and in everything that I do. When our intentions are pure, other things tend to fall in line. In high school, I felt isolated even though I had a decent group of friends and associates. This was part of my life that I wish I could have passed altogether, but hey, you live, and you learn. Even in these times I still knew what my purpose was and reluctantly I started my educational journey at South Carolina State University. My mother was more intent on my going to college then I was. She dropped me off a week prior to the start of classes. As a college freshman, I was not excited about it, but as you get older you realize that things do happen for a reason. Going to college was one of the BEST things that ever happened to me. I was blessed to have several mentors and professors with their doctorates.

It was not until I became a graduate student that I realized the value of South Carolina State University. Attending a Historically Black College or University (HBCU) was extremely beneficial to my personal growth. There is something about an HBCU that cannot be found anywhere else. I learned things that were not taught in high school. South Carolina State University taught me how to be an independent thinker, understand historical facts about our culture, and create greatness. I remember my first encounter and conversations with my professors. Four African Americans, two males and two females—all doctors—sparked a fire in me that I did not know existed. Professors like Dr. Staten, Dr. Washington, Dr. Hollis-Staten, and Dr. Maultsby encouraged me to strive for more and NEVER settle. I graduated with honors, obtaining my Bachelor's in 2008. Still struggling with returning to school after being offered a full ride to get my Masters, I decided to enter the workforce. I got a job with the State of South Carolina as an administrative assistant. At one point I considered the military as an option; however, this opportunity was not what I thought it would be. Before shipping out to basic that November, I decided to accept that full ride waiting for me at SC State. Reaching back to my former professor, I was able to return to South Carolina State to complete my Master's in Counseling in 2012. This is where I focused my attention on doctoral programs. I considered the University of South Carolina, but by that time I was living in Pennsylvania, so it only made sense to attend school there. I found a great program at Drexel University that offered a concentration in Higher Education and a flexible schedule, allowing me to work. I spoke with a few mentors and family members about my plans. They all encouraged me to apply. Unbeknownst to me, I got accepted into the program the summer of 2013 to begin classes in the fall.

Though Drexel University is a Predominately White Institution (PWI), there was not much of a culture shock coming from an HBCU. When I started the program, I was the only African American female in a cohort of ten. The cohort consisted of two black males, one white male, and six white females. I tried to ignore the fact that I was the "only" one. I later got close to one of the white females and the white male; however, they both dropped the program. I could feel the differences from the first day of class. This program made me realize that "*all skin folk ain't kin folk*." One of the black males made a comment about dating and companionship. He told me that because I was a black female with a doctoral degree, that it would be hard for me to date and that my chances of marriage were slim. His statement made me question his reason(s) for saying what he said because he was not married to a woman that resembles my complexion or educational achievement. It was funny that a man that resembles me in complexion will make such a comment that it will be hard for me, but he wouldn't date me either because of those same reasons. This is why it is so important to believe in yourself and not allow others to determine how you feel about yourself. This built my confidence even more and to NEVER settle. The division of course was not shocking to me, just from my observations and through conversations. I had no desire for acceptance. I think independently of others and that is a gift. The only time I really got any conversation from the males in my program occurred when things were not going well for them or if they wanted me to stand with them on a specific issue related the program. Whenever my black male counterparts would speak in class, people would listen and engage, but when I spoke you could hear a pin drop and no one responded. I also had to deal with the disrespect of a professor that turned his back to me while lecturing, only speaking to the white females as he taught. To make matters worse, when I asked to speak with him about a few assignments that we had disagreements about, he refused to speak to me. I felt more and more isolated and just decided to sit back and speak less. Not only did I feel things getting difficult in my educational journey, but it became more real outside of my educational experience.

Once again life happened, and I felt so much loss hit me all at once. I lost my three-year relationship with my then ex-fiancé, lost my baby brother, and I almost lost my mind when I found out that my mom had been diagnosed with breast cancer in the Fall of 2013. I moved back home to take care of my mom and my brother, while flying back and forth to school in Pennsylvania once a month. I was also working full-time and had a part-time job on the side. I felt like quitting the program and came close to it. My mother told me that quitting was not an option. While holding a conversation with my brother one day at the hospital, he told me how important it was that I finish what I started and that I needed to appreciate every moment. He also told me that I had to LIVE, and I am keeping that promise!

A doctoral degree is an achievement on a level by itself. People think that doctors are arrogant, and, believe me, some are; however, others wonder why I am so humble. Like I always tell people, "I make the degree, it does not define me." The real purpose of the doctorate was far bigger than me. I promised my mother and my brother that I would finish. I knew that education was a vital part of what I needed to do to walk in my purpose. I could remember having this conversation with my grandmother. She was very influential in my upbringing and, although she was not well educated, she was very wise, and I respected and admired her strength very much. Education was a big priority to her. She raised nine children while maintaining a household, working as a domestic and running a business with my grandfather. The stories she told me about her experiences influenced my decisions to work in the community and help others. Working in the criminal justice field also inspired me to get my degree to make changes in policy and to give people hope. I witnessed the differences in how black children were judged and sentenced differently than other children for the same crime(s). After working as a Probation Officer, I started working in the counseling field. As a counselor, I worked with different types of people daily struggling with mental health issues and other challenges. Counselors provide support and their passions are often rooted in helping others. My purpose was just that, to serve others. Someone once told me that I could not save everybody. My response to that was, "If I reach just one, I have done my duty." In my current position as a Director, I am extremely excited to shape young minds and create opportunities for young adults that they might not have gotten otherwise. As a professional and a young doctor, I use my platform as an example for my students, especially students of color. These experiences led me to my professional journey to work with youth.

Professional Experiences: The Finish Line...Please Allow Me to Reintroduce Myself

Professional experiences prepared me for my career and my purpose. Working in state government and in institutions of higher learning, I had the opportunity to establish myself as an expert in workforce development and entrepreneurship. As I have mentioned before, all things happen for a reason, and although we may not understand it at the time, we need to be prepared. A doctoral degree can play a vital role in how people perceive you. Some people are unable to handle our accomplishments despite our humbleness. I have been disrespected by White counterparts, Latino, and, not surprisingly, by people that look like me.

I finished third in my cohort for a successful defense. I had announced the accomplishment, "Please allow me to reintroduce myself...I am now Dr. Scott." There were people that were happy for me and others not so much. One of my students found out that I was a doctor and couldn't believe it. He referenced a White older male as someone that he thinks of when he hears the word "doctor." I did not take offense, but he was very excited about my accomplishment. I have encountered many instances in which the *doctor* in my professional title has not been respected or well-received. I can only assume that it comes with my age, gender, and race. As a person that does her job well, there are times when people will "test your gangsta!" Meaning many people will test you and do things purposely in attempt to take you out of your element or character. I have had several situations where I have had to maintain my composure. I had one supervisor threaten to fire me when I was a counselor because she said that I disrespected her in front of other staff. Days later, I was called into her office for my review. She put her hands up as if she were going to discipline me, telling me that I had to answer her when she asked a question. I told her that nonverbal communication is a form of communication. I did not raise my voice and remained calm but in my mind I was ripping her apart.

Sometimes people want to get a rise out of you and giving them the opposite of what they expect throws them completely off. Some people can afford to be unprofessional because they are protected by who they know and not what they know.

I stress the importance of who you know, not what you know, to my students. But I also let my students know that it is best if you know who you know and know what is required of you to know. While working for another college in Atlanta, I was introduced to Dr. Florence Ferguson. I was able to learn so much from her due to her expertise in higher education. With her support, and the support of another influential figure throughout my program, Dr. Joyce Pittman, I was able to focus and move forward with my dissertation. These women experienced so many gender and racially based microaggressions. These microaggressions occur when people do not "think" you are supposed to be a doctor because you do not "look" like a doctor. I had such supportive friends, mentors, and family that pushed me to excel. There is something about black women standing together through difficult times. We band together even when we face opposition. Many people in positions of leadership are not genuine in what they do or even care enough to understand that their decisions adversely affect the outcomes for everyone.

Over the course of my professional career and since I completed my doctoral degree, I have faced many issues with opposition from supervisors, staff, and even some students. People expect that because of my age, race, and gender, I should not be a doctor. My experiences with supervisors have been challenging at times but it has taught me lessons like how to work for micromanagers or difficult people. I have had supervisors talk to me like I am a child or try to make me feel less because of my degree. I just know that this is not the end of my journey. My passion is going to put me where I am meant to be. I am extremely passionate about working with students, social justice, and change. The decision to focus my study on prisoner reentry and education gave me a platform to start speaking at a national level. My dissertation focused on the incarceration of African American men and challenges associated with reentry. My work has been well received at professional conferences across the county including the prestigious Columbia University. I am currently working on writing articles on the subject. I am also preparing to establish my counseling practice to serve those in the community struggling with mental health and other issues.

There is a level of responsibility that comes with this degree. It is not enough to just have it, but to do the work to change people's lives.

The doctoral experience has truly impacted my professional relationships because of outright disrespect where people will purposefully downplay my accomplishments. I know who I am, and because people call me by my first name, that does not change who I am or what I have accomplished. There are times when I have felt alone, but I know that other black women deal with these same feelings from conversations such as being passed over for promotions and/or feeling like we are unable to speak our mind for fear of being labeled the "angry black woman." From coursework to the personal and professional experiences, we will be tested at every turn. There are good things that come from our experiences and our challenges, as these things are designed to build us up.

Conclusion & Closing Thoughts

African American women represent and penetrate many professional platforms. We are often overlooked or not given the proper respect we deserve. Such examples can be seen in the movie, "*Hidden Figures*" where African American women were mathematically inclined to plot the trajectory of a vessel around the earth. Some of the numerous contributions made by black women throughout history is always hidden from sight. The good thing about this program is that it taught me how to become more powerful and confident in my self-worth. It is beneficial to have support and people that are *genuinely* in your corner. I was blessed to have several friends in Pennsylvania, South Carolina, and Georgia. All these 'sistas,' with respect, confidence, and professionalism supported me throughout my journey.

My words of advice are to avoid people that are not for you. You will eventually find out who these people are. With growth comes change. As you grow, people will either grow with you or move on…LET THEM! Another important thing to remember is to take care of yourself first, whether that is listening to music, exercising, or just taking a break from your dissertation. I put God first and continued to pray throughout my process. There will be times when you will want to give up. It is just part of the process, so TRUST HIM! That is How I Got Over because I did not grow remaining in comfortable situations. That is the Power in My Purpose!

About Dr. Pia L. Scott

Dr. Pia L. Scott is a native of Charleston, South Carolina and currently resides in Atlanta, Georgia. She is the manager of College-to-Career programs and adjunct professor for a large research institution. She is the CEO and founder of CareerLit Consulting Services which provides small business development consulting and other services for transitioning veterans, formerly incarcerated, and professionals. Pia attended South Carolina State University where she received her Bachelor's in Criminal Justice and Masters in Rehabilitation Counseling. She completed her Doctorate in Educational Leadership & Management with a focus in Higher Education from Drexel University after successful defense of her dissertation titled, "African American Men Speak: Unheard Perspectives of the Self-Paced In Class Education Program (SPICE) and Reentry in the 21st Century."

Her dedication to her scholarly work has resulted in professional presentations at the prestigious Columbia University and other national conferences focused on prisoner reentry and the School-to-Prison-Pipeline. She has held leadership roles while in school and is currently the Director of Planning & Procurement for The Beverly Cunningham Outreach Program, a non-profit organization dedicated to providing access to healthcare, workforce development, and other resources to support the community. With a passion for working with youth, she volunteers her time educating and working with youth through the nonprofit Creating Our Future, Inc.

She is a Licensed Professional Counselor in the State of South Carolina and will be licensed in the State of Georgia. She is passionate about issues such as mental health, HIV, and human trafficking that impact the community. As a certified Global Career Development Facilitator, Pia provides training for career counselors and other professionals through workshops, seminars, and speaking engagements. She is the founder of Seth's Heart Foundation in memory of her brother who died from Leukemia at the age of 24. She is featured in The Drexel University Alumni Spotlight of the EdD Quarterly Newsletter recognizing her accomplishments. She embarks on a career of teaching, mentoring, and counseling in a variety of settings from human services, education, and state governments.

Pia's passion is clearly evident through her service, dedication, and purpose in serving others.

MEDICAL

Dr. Thea Barton

Dr. Yavetta Wood

Dr. Tiffany Middleton

Dr. Katrina Richmond

Dr. Elizabeth Holder

Dr. Thea Barton

"My precious child, I love you and would never leave you. During your times of trials and suffering, when you see only one set of footprints, it was then that I carried you."-excerpt from Footprints Poem

Mind over Matter....by God's Grace
By: Thea Cooper Barton, DO, FACOOG

Introduction

I grew up in a predominantly white, middle-class, suburb of Philadelphia during the 80s and 90s. I was certainly aware of my ethnicity, as well as, the lack of diversity in the area where I was raised, but nonetheless, I excelled both academically and socially. My leadership ventures began in 1985 when I was elected as President of the elementary school that I attended. Again in eighth grade, I was elected Student Council President. And finally, in my senior year, I served as the female Class President at the co-ed boarding school that I graduated from in 1993. My grandparents and parents were college graduates, so matriculation to college was not only celebrated but also, expected. My quest to become a physician, however, was uncharted territory, as I was the first in the family to embark on such a journey.

Personal Experiences

Education was the focus of my upbringing, as my mother was a pioneer in Special Education and my father in corporate America. As an only child, my parents were the main influences on my exposure to the world. I went to the best schools and traveled often. By all accounts, I grew up with a "silver spoon in my mouth." For most, I *should* be where I am in life. It is my own personal experiences, however, that made the journey much more complicated. After marrying my soul-mate at the young age of twenty-four, I started medical school in 1999. I tackled each topic, each course, each obstacle, just as I had done all my educational years, and prevailed. I was elected as Class President and served for four years. I received the Dean's Award at graduation. I matched into the OBGYN residency of my choice in 2003. By 2004, during my internship, I became pregnant with my first child. A daughter, Mackenzie Rayne, born September 3, 2004, six weeks early. I had endured the grueling focus of medical school, embarked on developing my craft, was five years into a solid marriage, and now, I became a mother. My life was grand. I was whole. I had my career and had my family. And, I was only *twenty-nine years old*. Little did I know -- the *journey* had just begun.

Professional Experiences

In January of 2004, I was in a terrible car accident on my way to work. Two weeks later, I began to experience numbness in my left upper extremity. My primary care physician ordered an MRI of my neck to see if I had a herniated disk during the accident. Unfortunately, it wasn't that simple. At 7:00 on a Wednesday morning, he called to say that the MRI results were much more concerning and that he wanted me to see a Neurologist. Being that I was a resident, getting time off was nearly impossible. Nonetheless, I met with the Neurologist within the next four weeks. More tests were run, more blood work obtained. Then, eleven days after my thirtieth birthday, on May 15, 2005, the diagnosis came. I had Multiple Sclerosis (MS). As if that weren't enough, I was told that I would never be able to endure the lifestyle of an Obstetrician and Gynecologist, as I needed as much rest as possible. I was strongly advised to change my specialty to accommodate this need. All that I had endured thus far -- the numerous trials and tribulations? Were they for not? I *couldn't, wouldn't,* and *didn't* believe that God had brought me this far, only to have me turn away from my purely God-given ability to help bring life into the world.

For months, I secretly wallowed in despair as I felt my personal world crashing down around me. While I started treatment immediately, getting used to the medication was quite the challenge. The weekly injection made me feel like I had the flu and the steroids made my heart pound out of my chest. All the while, I never missed a day of work. I thrived professionally as I was able to focus on the needs of my patients, and not on my own ailment. When home, I pushed past the pain to avoid neglecting my husband and my young child. All the while, I felt like I was dying inside, slowly but surely.

Nevertheless, my faith continued to flourish. In my frequent moments of darkness, I felt God's love. With each delivery, each patient, each family, I felt His presence. I began to believe, truly believe, that this was the path that He had chosen for me. Through perseverance, I became enlightened. This wasn't *my* journey, but *His* journey for me.

By God's grace, in September 2005, I went into remission. My symptoms were finally more tolerable. I was weaned off the steroids and was left with the weekly injection. The painful injections would become the mainstay of my regimen in the daily battle against MS. There was no cure in sight and the science demonstrated that interferon injections could prevent relapses. It was my only hope. Shortly thereafter, we received a gift from God -- I was expecting a second daughter. Kennedy Elle was born into our family on July 11, 2006. I felt whole again. I was Chief Resident as a third-year, I had come to terms with my diagnosis, and I was determined to never let MS derail my spirit. Again, little did I know?

Kennedy was thirteen months when my second flare occurred. This time I was crippled. Fortunately, I responded to grueling steroid treatment but was advised to avoid future pregnancies. Pregnancy is associated with relapses for some women with MS. Once again, my world started to crumble. I had always wanted three children and struggled with the recommendation that I should not conceive again. Unfortunately, I was faced with the notion that extending our family could risk the possibility of deficits from which I could not recover.

I graduated from residency in 2008 and began my internship as an employed physician for a non-profit organization. Eighteen months into the journey, the organization decided to close the obstetrical unit and I was forced to find a new job. I landed with a two-partner, private practice not far from home and thought this move would be magical. They had children the same ages as mine and were looking for a team player who could balance professional and personal life. Where do I sign? Quickly I realized, however, that I was the only team player who showed up for the game. For ten years prior to my arrival, the two of them had endured such grueling schedules that it was time for me to "pay my dues." As medicine is a hierarchy, the junior associate in the practice doesn't have much input or opinion. I lived on the Labor and Delivery Floor days on end. I didn't see my family. I couldn't complain to my parents. There was no "1-800" number to call. My joints ached from not resting enough. I cried in the parking lot and on my way in. I couldn't let my patients see my pain and I wouldn't let my family know the depth of my suffering. The car was my only private solace. Could they have been right? Could I not tolerate the lifestyle of an OBGYN? Despite the darkness, I remained focused on the journey He had for me. I knew that if I endured my three-year obligation to the community, He would open yet another door for me to walk through.

In 2013, I returned to my previous employer to focus on Gynecology Surgery. I explained to my patients that "I stopped delivering babies because I love my babies more." My patients are women. They are mothers who understood my core. I needed a lifestyle that would help me balance the demands of both my career and motherhood. Furthermore, I knew physically I would get more rest, as surgical emergencies occur far less than obstetrical urgencies. I would be able to restore and rejuvenate more frequently, and most importantly, more consistently.

In 2016, I finally felt like I was coasting, when suddenly my employment was in jeopardy when a for-profit organization purchased the hospital. Although monetarily enticing, I declined a lateral move to a distinguished hospital-system in the area. My inner voice, the voice that I now know to be His, urged me in a different direction. And so, I followed that voice -- I took a leap of faith. I successfully opened my own private practice specializing in Gynecology and Gynecologic Surgery. I never would have imagined twenty years ago, that in my early 40s, I would be in this position today. Although the journey was arduous, it is clear that each and every step prepared me to have the courage and wisdom to believe in Him, and myself.

Conclusion and Closing Thoughts

In conclusion, I reflect on a question posed in the poem, *Footprints: Why do I only see one set of footprints in the sand?* The answer is quite profound. "My precious child, I love you and would never leave you. During your times of trials and suffering, when you see only one set of footprints, it was then that I carried you." This journey is certainly not one I expected to endure while growing up with that *silver spoon*. Every obstacle that I was faced with, prepared me for the life that God envisioned for me. I would never have had the courage to pursue private practice had I not walked the path that He laid before me. It is my faith in God that has allowed me to persevere. I have been in remission for eleven years, so I no longer look at my diagnosis as a hindrance. Instead, it was a *blessing*. My good days are *great* and my *great* days are spectacular. As I learned early on in the disease process, I focus on the needs of my patients, and not on my own ailment. I hone in on positive energy and it radiates from my entire being. I know that it is God's light shining through me. My patients can see it. It sets me apart. They say it's 'mind over matter' but I call it...*by God's grace.*

About Dr. Thea Barton

Dr. Thea Cooper Barton is a Board Certified gynecologist who has been practicing since 2003. Dr. Barton was born in West Chester, Pennsylvania and graduated from Westtown School. From there, she attended the University of Virginia and received a Bachelor of Arts in English Literature. In 1999, Dr. Barton began her journey in medicine at the Philadelphia College of Osteopathic Medicine. She completed her internship and residency at Mercy Suburban Hospital in Norristown, Pennsylvania. For the past fifteen years, Dr. Barton has been connecting with women, not only on a professional basis but also on a personal level, as she is both wife and mother. She can relate to the current demands of a woman and understands the effects that can have on, not only the physical state but the mental state as well.

Dr. Barton focuses on the 'whole patient' approach to assess symptoms and to identify the cause of and/or contributing factors in regards to a woman's gynecologic issue(s). Not only is she an expert on Polycystic Ovarian Syndrome (PCOS) but she also specializes in minimally invasive laparoscopic and robotic surgery to cure common conditions such as fibroids and endometriosis. Dr. Barton has a special passion for treating the adolescent population. She believes that healthy gynecologic lifestyles can be nurtured during the teenage years and fostered into adulthood.

Currently, Dr. Barton is the owner of Progressive Gynecology in East Norristown, Pennsylvania. She has been married for 20 years and has two teenage daughters. When not focusing on her thriving practice, Dr. Barton enjoys hanging out with her bullmastiff (Gus), traveling, and entertaining with family and friends.

Dr. Yavetta Wood

"Life for me ain't been no crystal stair. It had tacks in it, splinters, boards torn up, and places with no carpet on the floor." ~Langston Hughes

Regardless of The Storms, Only You Can Change Your Life

By: Dr. Yavetta Wood-Robinson

Introduction

I grew up in Philadelphia in a single parent household from the ages of nine until seventeen. Prior to this, I lived with my grandparents. They were loving and supportive in every way. We were not rich, but I certainly never wanted for anything when I lived with them. My grandmother named me, which is interesting when I think of the bond that we always had, indeed God sent me an angel.

She was an amazingly proud woman, who was always so giving to others. She taught illiterate adults and special education. My grandfather worked as a cook but also served as the cook of our household. It was only after he died, that I learned he was illiterate. It was his illiteracy that drove my grandmother to pursue her specific career path. She was featured in local magazines and newspapers for her work, while my grandfather couldn't even read the publications.

From a very young age, she instilled in me the importance of education. I remember going to award dinners where she was the honoree and beaming with pride that she was my grandmother. The way people looked at her with admiration and respect left me in awe. She showed me that through hard work and determination, anything is possible.

Personal Experiences

My life changed quite drastically when I moved in with my mother. In less than a year of my move, my grandfather was dead, and I was in a new school with new surroundings. Looking back on that time, I realize I must have been in shock. All of those changes at once was too much for a nine-year old to comprehend. I rebelled against my mother; her rules, her just not being my grandmother. She had quite a different way of parenting that I wanted no part of. I missed my "old normal" desperately. Nonetheless, I focused on what I did have control over, and that was my education.

I had always been an avid learner and I didn't let a change in environment affect my studies. I worked hard in school, won several academic awards in high school, became inducted into the National Honor Society, and successfully competed in many science fairs. I graduated high school in the top 10 percent of my class but found myself struggling a bit during my first couple of months in college. Going to college was more than expected by my grandmother, while my mother, however, was not too happy about the idea. She felt that at seventeen years old, I was too young to go away from home. Eventually, I found my stride in college and after my freshman year, I was on the Dean's list every semester. While I was excelling in school, my personal life was difficult at best. I did not have much monetary support and aside from my grandmother and a mentor, there was no emotional support to be had either. I made ends meet by living off student loans and taking campus jobs. I refused to take my eyes off my goal to be the first person in my family to graduate from college. My strength was tested during winter break of my junior year. My grandmother had been diagnosed with Multiple Myeloma a few years prior, and while I knew her condition was getting worse, I had no idea it would be terminal. She died while I was on my way to see her.

My mother received the call from my aunt who was caring for her. Neither shared the news with me before I left the house. I arrived to find my grandmother cold; I just couldn't believe she was gone. I actually had a psychological break of sorts, refusing to let the mortician take her body initially. I was so angry with my mother, my aunt, and God. How could this happen? Why didn't I know that her condition was terminal? Did she know? I blamed myself initially for not researching Multiple Myeloma more. Why didn't I ask her doctor if she was dying? I trusted everything my grandmother said. She never spoke of the pain she was in every day, she never spoke of her mortality, she, in fact, had been preparing to take classes at community college. I interpreted this as her not knowing she was dying and somehow her doctors were at fault for not telling her that her condition was terminal. It was at that moment, I decided I was going to be the doctor I believed she didn't have.

Winter break ended, and I returned to campus a completely different person. I changed my major from Chemistry to Biology to the shock of my advisor and friends. I no longer wanted just to be the first person in my family to graduate from college, but now I wanted to be the first Doctor in my family as well.

When it came time to apply to medical school, I decided that I only wanted to apply to schools in Philadelphia. After losing my grandmother, I wanted to be in closer proximity to my family. Against all odds, I applied to only one medical school. This is not the norm, nor do I encourage anyone to do it. My college had a premedical committee that only met several times a year, and ironically regardless of how stellar of a student I was and how often I would see committee members (as they were my college professors) this meeting kept getting rescheduled by them. When I finally had the meeting, I remember being asked repeatedly why I wanted to go to medical school? If I was sure I understood what that would entail? I left my committee meeting with the green light to apply but doubting myself as well.

Professional Experiences

My time in medical school was eye-opening, to say the least, however, I excelled and even won several academic awards. During various rotations, I found that I had a keen interest in primary care. After graduation, I matched into a Family Practice residency in Columbus, Georgia. I rotated there several times as a fourth-year medical student, and I absolutely fell in love with the people, the program, and the weather. It was the farthest I had been from home in, but I felt the fit was right for me. I completed my internship year and decided that while I loved primary care, I only wanted to care for adults. I transferred from that program into an Internal Medicine Residency in New Jersey. I completed my residency in 2008. My first couple of months as an attending physician was challenging and pretty scary, to say the least. In residency, there is always at least a few people to bounce off your ideas about a particular diagnosis or treatment regimen. As a senior resident, while you are given a great deal of autonomy and responsibility, you ultimately still have an Attending physician that ultimately has the final say. I knew being the sole one to make all decisions would take some getting used to. What I didn't expect was to have some of my decisions, or thoughts downright second-guessed and at times completely disregarded by some others attending and even some nurses. When you are an Intern or Junior Resident it was not uncommon to have senior house staff and at least one nurse question your every move or thought. I considered this to be a rite of passage during training, and yes there were times when I felt it was probably a little more, but I brushed it off, maybe even expected it. As a woman of color, I knew too well what it felt like to the only person in the room that looked like me. I also knew that I had to work twice as hard at everything. Even with this knowledge and experience, I was still not expecting some of the unsavory behavior that I encountered as a new Attending. I realized that regardless of the reasons, how I dealt with these behaviors would become just as important. I had to remember my goal, walk in my purpose and most importantly remind myself that I was "enough" and capable of succeeding in this new phase of my career with or without pleasantries at the nurse's station or in the Doctors lounge. With time everything improved, and I developed friendships and professional relationships that continue to this day.

I now work exclusively in the hospital setting, which allows me to interact with my patients sometimes multiple times a day and obtain important test results quickly to further guide care. The road to becoming a Medical Doctor has been long, yet so very rewarding. I am so humbled by the opportunity that I have been given to positively affect the lives of others.

Conclusion & Closing Thoughts

Today as I look back on my journey, I remember being that soft-spoken girl who just wanted to make her grandmother proud. I've always loved the poem from Langston Hughes, "Mother to Son" that I included in the beginning of this chapter. This poem has always spoken to me because I've always seen my story intertwined within this beautiful piece. There were indeed times when I felt as though the stairs that I needed to climb had nails or splinters along the way, making my gait appear painful but never did I stop climbing. I now know that my grandmother was undoubtedly told about her terminal condition, but she did not want me to know. She to her last breath put my needs before hers. I take pride in knowing that I kept my promise to my grandmother, for it is her face that I see in every patient that I treat. I sincerely believe that through hard work and perseverance anything is possible. Never give up on your dreams no matter how difficult obtaining them may seem.

About Dr. Yavetta Wood

Yavetta Wood is a native of Philadelphia, Pennsylvania. Dr. Wood received her medical degree from Philadelphia College of Osteopathic Medicine and is Board Certified in Internal Medicine.

Dr. Wood has been dedicated to the delivery of comprehensive medical care to hospitalized patients for the past 10 years.

Dr. Tiffani Middleton

"Success is not final, failure is not fatal: it is the courage to continue that counts."
~Winston Churchill

Get Up and Keep Moving
By: Dr. Tiffani M. Middleton

Introduction

My name is Tiffani M. Middleton, MD and I am a practicing Obstetrician/Gynecologist in Baltimore, MD. The above-mentioned quotes are special to me because at various points on my journey to becoming a physician, each one of them helped to encourage me and gave me that extra boost I needed at the time to stay in the race. To this day, whether I'm speaking with a colleague or a patient regarding a difficult situation, I always try to encourage them by saying: "You've got to get up and start moving. Keep putting one foot in front of the other, and soon this too shall pass."

Personal Experiences

There is usually one defining moment when a person discovers his/her calling. For me, it occurred while I was in middle school, during visits with my younger cousin, ChiLaine Jenkins, while she was hospitalized due to leukemia. At the time, I did not fully understand the severity of her illness, nor the impact her death would have on me or our family. I recall feeling helpless during her illness. But I also remember some of her physicians and their interactions with her and the family. They were caring, intelligent, and relatable. I remember thinking: "This is what I want to do- I want to help people get well!"

Once I decided I wanted to be a physician, I made every effort to participate in activities that would give me more exposure to the medical field. While in high school, I volunteered during summer breaks as a candy striper in a local hospital. My duties included: working at the Information Desk and Gift Shop; running errands for different departments; and, assisting with flower deliveries to the patients. However, my most favorite tasks included operating the Book Mobile. For those of you who remember prior to digital books, people had to travel with hard copies (i.e. an actual book). The Book Mobile was similar to a traveling library. Volunteers would push a cart full of novels and magazines door-to-door to different patients' rooms, allowing them the opportunity to check-out reading material. In the grand scheme of things, these were very simple tasks. However, the satisfaction I experienced while performing these small acts of comfort to patients further solidified my desire to become a physician.

While at the University of South Carolina- Columbia, I majored in biology. It was not only a subject I found interesting, but I knew that it would also help me further my goals of becoming a physician. It was during this time that I met some of my life-long friends. Many of those friendships were congealed over numerous all-night study sessions and our individual desires for a profession in the health/medical field. We not only encouraged each other during low points but also celebrated our successes. While in college, I worked as a data-entry specialist for an insurance company. It was interesting to see the vast differences in insurance plans and their coverages. From this experience, I received my first introduction into the business aspect of medicine. I learned the importance of proper coding for reimbursement for physicians, but also the importance of proper insurance coverage for patients.

After college graduation, I found myself in a unique position. As a December graduate, I did not have a solid plan for my next step. I just knew I wanted to go to medical school. However, admissions only occur in the fall. So, I returned home to Charleston and worked a series of temporary jobs. I worked as an office assistant, daycare teacher, and jewelry store clerk. All this time, I was taking classes at local colleges on my own that I thought would later be helpful to me in medical school. I took classes like Histology and Physiology at the College of Charleston. During this time, I received my certification as an Emergency Medical Technician. I also took preparatory classes for the Medical College Admission Test (MCAT). Everything I did was in preparation for medical school.

So what do you do when things don't work out the way you envisioned? You keep trying, and that's exactly what I did! I did not get into medical school during my first attempt. Interestingly enough, there are many of us out there with similar stories. But I can only elaborate on mine. I was disappointed, disheartened, and sometimes angry. But I did not allow sentiments of hopelessness and despair to fester. I just figured it was not my time. I had to trust and believe that if this calling was meant for me, as long as I walked in faith and did my part, God would provide. So, I kept getting up! It was during this time that I started working as a Research

Associate. Surprisingly, I started at the Medical University of South Carolina about the same time as my good friend from college, now Dr. Rivers. We both studied for the MCAT together and supported each other in our pursuit of medicine. My boss, Dr. Means, Jr. was instrumental in helping me navigate the medical school application process. He encouraged me by allowing flexibility in my schedule so that I could take classes. He also provided solid advice with regards to the medical school application and interview process. When it came time for my decision regarding medical school, he was very influential in helping me make the decision to remain at home in Charleston, at the Medical University of South Carolina.

So now you'd think: "Ok, she made it to medical school, end of story." But that is far from the case. Once I was accepted into medical school, then came another adjustment period. Like many before me, I had to figure out a different way to study: I needed to review, process, and retain large amounts of information. Then I had to be able to apply it to different patient scenarios. Someone once described studying in medical school as standing in front of a fire hose with your mouth open. You just want a drink of water, but you're about to drown from the force and volume of the water in the fire hose. The amount of information is taught in medical school is just that vast. The first two years provide the foundation of basic knowledge with structured classes. This prepares students for the second two years, clinical studies, where they are exposed to the different medical disciplines through rotations (Medicine/Pediatrics/Neurology/Surgery/Obstetrics & Gynecology/Psychiatry/etc.) prior to deciding on a specialty.

Like many others, I had to do a major overhaul with studying. This is where study groups and practice test questions become essential to success. The study group is helpful in several different ways: different people can provide different ways to memorize or comprehend information; topics can be broken up into smaller portions and each person can provide a summary/outline; and, it's nice to have a support group of people going through the same thing as you. Through these study groups, you also develop your networking skills. That networking comes in handy while on clinical rotations.

While at MUSC, I was assigned to a small group facilitated by the then Associate Dean of the College of Medicine, Dr. E.V. Del Bene. At that time, I remember being nervous because I wanted to just "stay under the radar," get my degree and be on my way. I did not know, but he was a music aficionado- specifically, the organ (pay attention). Also working at the university at the time as the Director of the Office of Diversity was one of my mother's college classmates, Dr. Bell. He, along with his office assistant, Mrs. Whittaker- who was one of my mother's former students- made certain to keep an eye out for me and other students to ensure we had what was needed for our success. Interestingly enough, prior to starting medical school, I started playing the organ for my home church (I told you to pay attention). The Rector of our church, the late Bishop Sanco K. Rembert, was good friends with the former president of the College of Medicine, Dr. Edwards.

I initially was skeptical and saw all these people/relationships as a negative thing. I kept thinking the universe had it out for me. All of these people would have a front row seat to see me fall on my face if I were not successful in my endeavors. Little did I know, when I encountered some of my darkest days as a student, these were the people who would be instrumental in encouraging me to continue to strive for my goals of becoming a physician. They had already seen my dedication and they knew my character. They helped keep me on track, but also encouraged me with their support. Although I wanted to do everything on my own, I realized with each of these relationships, that you never know how people/things are interrelated. Or simply put, it's best summarized by Romans 8:28: *And we know all things work together for good to those who love God and to those who are called according to His purpose.*

There is a saying that goes: treat everyone the way you would want to be treated. This is the way of the world. But it was never more evident than in the hospital setting. You never know how people are connected. I tried to be friendly/courteous to everyone with whom I came in contact- asking about a child that recently graduated or the family member that was ill. It didn't matter to me if the person was a patient, family member, nursing staff, cafeteria worker or housekeeper. I treated everyone the same. These are the people who would give me an extra helping of food during those late-night study sessions or make certain I had extra linen in the call rooms. In medicine, half of the battle is to know the most recent patient updates (labs/studies/status) before the resident and attending physicians. The nurses would make sure that I was aware of the patient's progress throughout the night, so I could give an accurate report to the resident and attending physicians. By doing this, they helped me to shine on my rotations.

I will be the first person to say that like many before and many after me, medical school was definitely a challenging time. However, I got through it and so will you! The first thing you should do is find your tribe. This is that group of friends who support you when you're down and celebrates with you when you're up. My tribe included: Dr. Caton (Internal Medicine), Dr. Haney-Singleton, (Ed.D.) (MUSC Associate Dean for Student Affairs and Student Wellness), Dr. Moore (Obstetrics/Gynecology), Dr. Paysinger (Pediatrics), Dr. Price (Rheumatology), and Dr. Richmond (PharmD). Keep in mind these were my friends **before** any of us obtained the titles. Most of the ladies, I met while we were each pursuing our professional degrees. These are the women I could call if I needed to study, take a break and grab something to eat, or just vent about life in general. Likewise, they could do the same with me. This was my tribe.

Once I graduated from medical school, life became a little easier for me. It's like I could take a deep breath. I moved to Baltimore, MD where I completed my residency in Obstetrics and Gynecology at Franklin Square Medical Center. There, it was just as much studying, but it was learning specifically about the care of women as it related to preventative care, contraception, pregnancy, non-pregnant conditions of women, etc. From the time I assisted with my first delivery of a baby, to the time I assisted with my first hysterectomy, I loved it! I knew in my soul, that I'd made the right choice. This is what I was meant to do, and where I was supposed to be. I must thank Dr. Bibum, my first Chief Resident. She lives up to her nickname, The Bibum-nator. She made certain that those under her knew our stuff.

Likewise, I have to thank the attending physicians who helped train me and all the other residents while at Franklin Square. Although there are too many to mention by name, I would be remiss if I didn't mention my former faculty advisor, Dr. London. She is the person who had the most influence on me while I was a resident. She made certain that I stayed focused on the demands of residency. But she also could be counted on to make certain that I knew the importance of having a life outside of work. She is now my boss at Women's Care OB/GYN.

It is not lost on me that I have the unique opportunity and privilege of being with people during some of the happiest moments of their lives. Just as important, I am also with patients during some of the most devastating periods that one can encounter. Even to this day, 10 years after graduating from residency, I am grateful for each and every opportunity that I have to be involved in the care of my patients. I know it would not have been possible had I stopped and given up with each setback I encountered during this journey. I'm glad that it was during those times, I relied on my faith and my family. This is when I kept one of my favorite scriptures in mind, Jeremiah 29:11. It motivated me to continue to get up and keep putting one foot in front of the other until those setbacks were stepping stones to my success.

Conclusion & Closing Thoughts

If I could give someone advice who wants to pursue medicine, the first thing I want you to know is, you cannot give up. Have a plan but be willing to revise the plan when necessary. While you are pursuing your destiny, there will be naysayers. **Pay them no attention**. From the time I was in high school until I graduated from medical school, there were people who did not think I could do it. They would say, "maybe you should think about doing something else," or "you still planning on being a doctor?" I remember one teacher in college who said he didn't think I'd make it in medical school-- said it to my face. All I can tell you, for whatever reasons those naysayers did not believe in me, I did not worry. It could have been my race, my gender, the fact that I was born in May. I didn't know, nor did I care. I just smiled and quietly continued doing what I needed to do to be a physician.

The one thing that's certain is: you have to keep going- never give up! The quote that "it's often darkest before the dawn" is true. I have always believed that only I and God can determine my destiny. When other people may have thought I was down and out, again, I did not worry about them or their opinions. As long as I did not believe it, that's all that mattered. For those times when doubt was clouding my judgment, I have to thank the people who kept me sane and pushed me forward: my parents- Seaward and Marguerite Middleton; my brothers- Rashard, Andre, and Larry; my close cousins Keturia Jenkins and Degwanda Smalls; and my close friends, Ailsa Emmel, Lissette Machin, Kimberly Mack-Washington, and Felicia Wright-Johnson. Lastly, I have to thank my aunts, uncles, cousins*, friends and New Israel Reformed Episcopal Church family who encouraged me throughout my journey. Your prayers and kind words have helped me get to where I am today. But I'm not done! Every day, I'm still putting one foot in front of the other; and, I'm certain that you will do the same as you pursue your goals. I look forward to working with you soon!

Special shout-out to my cousin, Pia who had the foresight to make this book a reality!

About Dr. Tiffani Middleton

Tiffani Marguerite Middleton was born to Seaward and Marguerite Middleton in Charleston, South Carolina. She was educated in Charleston County Public School System and was a graduate (of the first) Academic Magnet High School (Class) at Burke. After high school, she went on to graduate from the University of South Carolina where she obtained a Bachelor of Science in Biology. After working for a few years, Tiffani entered the Medical University of South Carolina and graduated with a Doctor of Medicine degree.

After completing a residency at Franklin Square Medical Center in Obstetrics & Gynecology, she worked at Women's HealthCare in Jacksonville, NC for five (5) years. She then returned to MD, where she works at Women's Care OB/GYN. She is board certified by the American Board of Obstetrics and Gynecology. She belongs to the following professional organizations: the American College of Obstetrics and Gynecology, National Medical Association, National Association for the Advancement of Colored People, and Alpha Kappa Alpha Sorority, Incorporated. During her spare time, Tiffani enjoys reading, bowling, traveling, and karaoke.

Dr. Katina Richmond

"Adversity causes some men to break; others to break records."
~William Arthur Ward

Life's Struggles Sharpen the Tools to Improve Your Life

By: Dr. Katina M. Richmond

Introduction

I was a shy girl from a very small town in South Carolina; the oldest of three children from the marriage of Joel W. and the late Jacqueline S. Richmond; a girl who often cried because she was teased for "acting white." I was raised to speak "proper English" and get good grades. But I wanted to be defiant – speak differently and alter my appearance so I could "just be like everyone else." But my mother rejected those notions. Instead, she spent extra time and often would remind me that I was intelligent and beautiful and that is was more than okay to simply be who God made me to be.

I grew up in a two-parent, two-person working, very modest, and humble home. It is fair to say that we pretty much lived paycheck to paycheck. We were loved by our parents and we had the majority of our needs and most of our wants provided. Please don't think that we never experienced a utility being disconnected for lack of payment, because we definitely did. We learned to be appreciative as well as the value of a dollar. Both of my parents were super supportive and encouraged us to do and be anything that we wanted to be. As the oldest child, I was expected to set the example. That meant, believe in God, act as if I had sense, give back to my community, and for heaven's sake, do not embarrass my parents.

Today, I am a proud graduate of two prestigious universities – Emory University in Atlanta, Georgia, where I hold a Bachelor of Science in Biology, and the Medical University of South Carolina in Charleston, South Carolina, with a doctorate in pharmacy (PharmD). I am one of only a handful of family members who have earned a four-year college degree and the first to earn my doctorate. I have the pleasure of working as a Registered Manager of General Operations (RMGO) and serving as a clinical pharmacist. And yet, I remain humbled by the experiences that have sharpened my tools in preparation of the journey that brought me to where I am today.

Personal Experiences: How did I get from here to there?

I have no memory of ever wanting to do anything other than to be a doctor. Why a doctor? Because we were taught to help others and that charity starts at home; and that we could be anything we wanted to be; and that medicine was a respectable line of work; and because I was inquisitive and a perpetual student who loved to learn new things. But most of all, it was expected of me. I was expected to work hard, be self- sufficient, keep the faith in our Heavenly Father, and make my parents proud.

From my parents' perspective, it was never a question of are you going to college, it was only a question of *where* you were going. So Why Emory? Because my mother felt my childhood dream school Boston University was too far, dad said to let her go, but mom was adamant. Thankfully, my high school guidance counselor, Mrs. Ollie Smith, introduced me to Emory University, "which is (known as) the Ivy League of the South," she noted.

With the application submitted, I visited the campus and fell in love with the school. Emory is located in Atlanta (a bit different from my small, rural hometown), and they had an amazing pre-med program. I already knew that I loved the two basic components of medicine – science and math – so of course pre-med was my best choice, right? Well, funny how life has a way of letting you know what you don't know. I quickly learned that I did not like the physiological aspects of medicine, things like blood, guts, and the overall gore of it all. So what now? All i ever wanted to be was a doctor, so now what?

I had to regroup. I sought the advice of my academic advisor, Dr. Marstellar, who lovingly, yet firmly, counseled me into a research position. I still vividly remember her saying, "You will NOT get a dead-end job," before offering me the name and number of one of her personal friends who happened to work in the field. And then she made me promise to get into a master's program to keep up my study skills. And so, I did.

I found a good job that paid the bills and did not take me too far from my degree and passion. I was working as a laboratory research specialist, feeling unfulfilled because this still did not feel like my passion. While grateful for the opportunity, I struggled to reconcile, again, doing what was expected of me, and what was right for me.

One day after work, I visited my local grocery store to fill a prescription when I looked up to see a young, African American female pharmacist. We began to chat, and her interest grew as she learned about my education and work experience. But when she asked if I had ever considered pharmacy, my answer probably shocked her as much as her response did me. "I have no desire to count pills all day," I quipped. I could tell she was determined to show me just how shallow my response was. Without skipping a beat, she responded, "Do you think that's all we do all day? Why don't you shadow me, and you'll see how pharmacists do so much more to impact the lives of our patients and improve the overall health of our communities."

The next week was extremely eye-opening. I shadowed this pharmacist as she counseled patients, compassionately educated them about the importance of medication adherence, liaised between patients and their health providers and served as a patient advocate. Specifically, I watched as she saved one patient's life by catching a potentially lethal drug-allergy interaction.

My understanding of "doctor" was transformed and my focus on becoming one was revived. I found my passion reignited. This – THIS – was my calling, my purpose. A few weeks later, I applied to pharmacy school at the Medical University of South Carolina, and a short time later, I was off to pharmacy school. I would soon (relatively speaking) be able to give back to my community, have a respectable career, and make my parents proud. My little girl dreams would finally be a reality and I would soon be a doctor.

Professional Experiences: Learning the Truth about Myself and the World

Starting out I was a young African American woman, often younger than the technicians and pharmacists around me. And some of my childhood fears seemed to pop back up in my new professional career. No, the kids weren't teasing me, but I soon noticed that I was often the unicorn in the room. The community in which I worked had not seen one like me before. At times, the racism was blatant, in-your-face hurtful, while other times I suspected or felt the covert racism but had no proof. I quickly learned that I had to not only earn but demand the respect of my colleagues and those I served. The best way I knew how to accomplish this was to revert to the teachings my parents and grandparents provided – keep your head down, work hard and let your work stand for itself. We were often told, "Get your education; that's the one thing they can't take away from you." Now more than ever that saying was more real than rhetoric. The solid ethics, values, and morals that I grew up with also would help shape how I responded to these challenges. These experiences would, yet again, force me to sharpen my tools.

I was appreciative of those colleagues and patients who loved me and learned to work with those who preferred I would disappear. I worked hard to learn as much as I could to eventually master my trade. Before long, opportunities began to arise where I could help train others and to open new stores. Leadership started to see my passion and ambition and recognize my strengths. I moved into management and leadership. I loved my work, which meant that it really wasn't work at all. My "work" was exciting and it motivated me to want to do more, learn more and grow more.

Naivety, however, was not a characteristic that I possessed. Trust was not a currency that I spent easily. I came to understand that everyone is not trustworthy and all that sparkles are not gold. Just because someone smiled in your face, does not mean that they aren't ready to place that knife in your back. Learning to determine who I could trust became just as important to advancing my career as maintaining my educational training. These incidents were hard life lessons that helped to sharpen my skills in discernment.

Conclusions and Closing Thoughts

Every experience in life teaches a lesson, and the lesson is dependent on what it is that you choose to learn. They build character and prepare you for the next challenge. Everything that you go through is intentional according to the life that is destined for you.

Over my lifetime I've learned that as you maneuver through challenges and work through the highs and lows, you must always look for the meaning of why this

challenge has been placed in your life. What is the lesson to take away? Yes, it may be painful and hurt like hell in the moment, but it is critical to reflect on what skill you sharpened and how you will let that experience make you a better person. My mother always told us that anything worth having is worth working and fighting for. If something comes too easily, you won't appreciate it.

In choosing a quote to represent this part of my life, the quote by William Arthur Ward resounds loudly as a reflection of my life: "Adversity causes some men to break; others to break records."

As a child, I wanted to fit in, but my parents taught me to stand out; I was to celebrate my differences and ultimately others would see the differences as an asset.

With the help and encouragement of my parents, I chose not to break. I got sharper.

As a college student, I learned that I couldn't live my life for others, because doing so was not living at all. Becoming a doctor was what I felt was expected of me. Once I realized that I had to decide for myself, I felt my stress level decrease, I found my own way and learned that healthcare was, in fact, where I wanted to be. From my shadowing experience with that pharmacist, I now knew that being a doctor didn't mean I had to be a medical doctor; a Doctor of Pharmacy really allowed me to use my math and science skills differently than what I originally considered. I chose not to break. I got sharper.

I have a passion for math and science, and I learned that pharmacy was where I could contribute to society. Through educating my community about managing their health, I satisfy my personal desire to give back. In the process, I was able to break a few records. While in pharmacy school I was elected the first African American female class president. I was notified by the local chapter of the NAACP where I began my pharmacy career, that I was the first African American female pharmacist in the county. I was the first in my family to achieve a doctorate degree. I launched a consulting business with a local university. I was the first pharmacist to teach pharmacology at a local community college.

I have been blessed to work with some truly amazing people who believed in me and encouraged me to be better and do bigger things. When I chose to step into my current role, I knew that I was stepping way outside of my comfort zone. I was taking on a new and different challenge: I had to learn a totally new aspect of the business, move to a new city, rebuild my network, and learn to work with different people, all while figuring out how to meet the expectations that were set for me. This was a new feeling for me because I've never had to wipe the slate clean and completely start from scratch. And now I had to do this all without the support of my greatest advocate who was no longer on this earth (we'd just lost my mother unexpectedly and now I had to draw on memories rather than call her for advice). I would have to figure out how to perform in a new role that I knew very little about, amongst people that I did not know. This new challenge was one I openly embraced, knowing my foundation was already laid; I would take one day at a time.

If I could offer advice to someone who looks like me, I'd offer the following: Remember that the decision to enter a doctoral program will most certainly be a challenge; a challenge that you can conquer. There will be wins, losses and everything between, so prepare to take the good with the bad. Trust and believe in yourself. Ensure that you have a solid support system. That support system will serve to keep you grounded, let you know when you are being ridiculous, pick you up when you fall down, encourage you when you don't understand why you started out on this crazy path and keep you on that path until you reach your destination. Choose wisely those in your inner circle. And most importantly, constantly reflect on your struggles because they do, in fact, provide opportunities to sharpen your skills and improve your life.

About Dr. Katina M. Richmond

A native of Moncks Corner, South Carolina, **Katina M. Richmond, PharmD**, was born the oldest of three children to Joel and Jacqueline Richmond. She graduated from Berkeley High School and went on to receive a Bachelors of Science degree in Biology from Emory University before attending a master's program at Emory University's School of Public Health. She later earned a doctorate in pharmacy from the Medical University of South Carolina.

Katina has held various positions over her more than 16-year career with Walgreens, ranging from staff pharmacist, pharmacy manager, Emerging Leader, clinical pharmacist and is currently a Registered Manager of General Operations (RMGO) for a Walgreens Specialty Pharmacy in Georgia. She oversees all operations of the pharmacy and front end of the store, including sales, staff, and stock and, most importantly, investigating financial assistance for patients' pharmaceutical needs. As one of only a handful of Utilization Review Accreditation Commission (URAC) pharmacies in the state, the standards are high and two aspects of her job that Katina loves most are mentoring staff and helping patients get the medications they need.

Katina enjoys leading community health and education events and has done so for more than 15 years. Her specific areas of interest are hypertension, oncology, diabetes, children's health, and women's health. She often presents at churches for vacation bible schools and educational weeks; youth groups such as YMCA's; career days at primary schools and colleges; and a variety of community events. Additionally, Katina visits health fairs providing blood pressure, blood glucose, and cholesterol screenings, as well as vaccination clinics.

Currently, Katina lives in Loganville, Georgia, just outside of Atlanta. She serves as a consulting pharmacist for both Student Health Services and the Athletic Department at Coastal Carolina University and a chiropractic office in South Carolina. She is a board member of The C.A.S.T. Coalition and CareTeam and a faithful member of Alpha Kappa Alpha Sorority, Incorporated.

Dr. Elizabeth Holder

"Greatness is not measured by what a man or woman accomplishes,
But by the opposition, he or she has overcome to reach his goals."-Dr. Dorothy Height

#TheEvolutionOfAPioneer
By: Dr. Elizabeth Holder

Introduction

Sirens, police cars, gun shots, drug deals, and teen pregnancy were all issues that plagued my North Philadelphia neighborhood growing up. Nevertheless, with strong Christian values and a phenomenal, resilient, and caring mother, I persevered. I am always reminded that it is by the Grace of God that I avoided those perils as a child.

My faith in Christ has kept me grounded over the years. One of my favorite scriptures is Jeremiah 29:11, "For I know the thoughts that I think toward you, saith the Lord, thoughts of peace, and not of evil, to give you an expected end." While my life is very short of being trial free, my faith in God's word reminds me that He has extraordinary work assigned to my hands. My faith coupled with my mother's desire for me to pursue a flourishing career have led me to this point in my life.

My mother received her high school diploma and entered into the workforce after high school. Like many single moms, who struggled to make ends meet, she aspired for me to reach heights that she did not have the opportunity to achieve. During the morning of March 6, 2017, my dream and my mother's hard work were fulfilled. In the presence of both my parents (step parents), committee members, and prospective doctoral students, I successfully defended my dissertation titled, "Career entry, retention, and advancement enablers and barriers for Black female nurses: An Interpretive study". I became Dr. Elizabeth Leah Holder. I not only became a doctor, but I received the university's highest honor, The Nicholas S. Rashford, SJ, Award for Outstanding Dissertation. This was a phenomenal accomplishment and a dream come true for my entire family.

In addition to obtaining my degree, I have been blessed with the opportunity to work in my "dream job" as the National Patient Experience Director for a Fortune 500 company. I work for a service organization that contracts with various healthcare organizations to improve patient satisfaction. My role within the organization is to strategize, develop, maintain service cultures, and partner with healthcare organizations in a way that creates positive experiences for patients and families. This is achieved through fostering strong relationships with hospital executives, front line managers, and nursing leadership to drive patient satisfaction outcomes within the hospital setting. The end goal for my organization and healthcare partners is to create hospital settings that draw a strong consumer base and drive strong financial gains.

While I carry letters behind my name, I will never neglect my experiences in my early beginnings. I, as Dr. Liz, would not be able to contribute in the life or in my career without my childhood experiences. They developed and shaped me into the woman that I am today.

Educational Experiences

As a child, I aspired to become a pediatrician. My initial major in undergrad was biology, but I decided to change because I did not perform well academically in the required science courses. I was discouraged and re-evaluated my career interests. I wondered if becoming a doctor was "out of reach". There was a period of time during my freshman year that I felt down and needed guidance. Through prayer and mentorship from various professors, my dreams of becoming a doctor were revitalized. Their recommendation led me to explore career opportunities where I could gain my doctorate degree in non-medical professions.

Fast forward to 2013, I was with my company for two years as a manager, and the desire to acquire a doctoral degree remained. I felt there was more to pursue. I believed a doctoral degree would prepare me for "greater works" in the job market and in the community.

What "greater works?", you may ask. I believed acquiring a doctorate degree was about doing something "greater". It wasn't about being called "doctor" but becoming a doctor would achieve two purposes: 1) I would position myself to help minority and underprivileged community members gain access to education and opportunity; and 2) I would pursue a career as a business strategist, assisting organizations to improve their processes, programs, and relationships. Once I identified that this was the direction that I wanted to pursue, it was time to search for the "perfect" program.

I did not want to pursue a traditional Ph. D., but I wanted to enroll in a program that would increase knowledge and develop practical skills simultaneously. One Sunday afternoon following morning church service, I had a conversation with a fellow member, who was in the process of completing the dissertation requirements at Saint Joseph's University (SJU). She and I discussed my education and career interests, and she recommended SJU's doctoral program.

Weeks later, I attended SJU's open house and participated in the Interdisciplinary Doctor of Education Leadership (IDEPEL) program's meet and greet information session. After the open house presentation, I was assured that this program best suited my interests. I believed this was true for several reasons:

- First, it was a program that would cultivate my qualitative/quantitative research skills. Research skills are critical to my ability to make decisions and provide insight to colleagues and clients as it relates to hospital patient satisfaction data and analysis.

- Second, the program is interdisciplinary, offering courses in quantitative/qualitative research, educational theoretical perspectives, leadership/organizational development, human/fiscal resources, law, and social policy. This vast course load formulated clear direction and perspective for my dissertation work.

- Third, it is a program that embodies Jesuit principles. As a Christian, many of the principles were applicable to my personal religious beliefs. The Jesuit values were interwoven throughout the coursework, guiding not only how students should lead within their respective organizations, but how they should live in harmony with others. In fact, this education changed my perspective on my role as a corporate leader and has influenced me to formulate a corporate community program for college and high school students in the Philadelphia area.

Life after my doctorate degree has been positive. My parents and siblings are extremely proud, and as a first generation college student, I am grateful that the Lord blessed me to accomplish such a feat. As for my "homegrown friends" (who have been through it all with me from childhood to present), they are ecstatic. They find every opportunity to introduce me as "Dr. Holder", especially if we are attending an event where such titles are held in high esteem (LOL…I love them!). And church family/friends, alike, have been congratulatory and supportive. I have been blessed with an all-around optimistic experience in this regard. In some instances, the reception in my professional experiences hasn't been welcoming.

Professional Experiences

As it relates to obtaining my doctorate degree, there have been mixed responses from my colleagues. On one hand, my manager and mentor with the company were excited and thought the idea of acquiring a doctorate degree would serve me well in the organization. They believed it would yield a high level of credibility from current and prospective clients; and based on recent experiences, their projection has been accurate.

Some colleagues, on the other hand, were not receptive (who was once an entry-level manager) about the doctorate degree. I believe they were uncomfortable with the notion that I would be perceived in a high regard within the organization. For example, my mentor sent an email to my colleagues informing them that I successfully defended my dissertation. The day following the defense one of my colleagues walked into the office and yelled "Oh, well hello Dr. Holder!" He frowned his face and walked into another office space. Moments later, the same colleague ranted that no one acknowledged his hard work. I ignored his comments and continued to work. However, I did experience an incident that "hit a nerve".

An adverse event with a colleague occurred one year prior to the defense. For the purposes of this chapter, I will call my colleague, "Thomas". Thomas projected himself as a trusted comrade; conversely, my intuition did not allow me to trust him because he made several attempts to undermine my leadership within the department. Thomas was a director in the department and would discuss information with the team regarding leadership changes. I received a promotion, and Thomas shared with my team that I accepted an advancement opportunity while going to school to receive my second "Master's degree". Thomas in past discussions shared that he did not believe that doctorate degrees (like PhDs or EdDs) warranted someone to be called "doctor".

His announcement bothered me. I felt that his statement was an attempt to diminish me as a person and a leader in the organization. At this point, I reached my limit with his ignorant rhetoric and dismissive behavior. So, on the same exact day he made the statement, I requested to speak with him. I calmly walked into his office and expressed my discontent with the information shared with the team regarding my educational pursuits. He interjected and said, "Liz, please don't be stupid enough to call yourself a "Doctor" when you are done."

I was visibly upset after this comment. I understood that leaving without a response would encourage him to repeat these negative statements in the future. So I took a deep breath and responded that "I would not allow him to marginalize me as a Black woman. I will call myself a doctor because I will become a doctor". I concluded my response by making him aware that he doesn't have the right to speak on my education because he is not familiar with the doctoral protocol. Before I exited his office, Thomas apologized.

Confrontation with these experiences was not easy to handle, however, it taught me the manner in which to verbally express my disgust while maintaining self-control. In the words of Michelle Obama, "When they go low, you go high." As Black women, I believe it is critical that we master high emotional intelligence and understand how to effectively articulate disapproval while preserving a calm demeanor. There are many times that we respond to situations and never achieve a resolve because we don't listen, our emotions take us over the ledge, and we fail to process the situation before we respond. Thinking before we speak or respond does make a difference. Fortunately, my circumstance resulted in an apology.

I believe that God allows things to happen in our lives for a reason. We have trials and confrontational experiences, similar to the ones shared earlier, to prepare and strengthen us mentally and experientially for our next assignment. I joined this company in 2011, and I have been promoted into two different roles. In 2015, my promotion was into a Patient Experience Manager role that did not exist for the organization, meaning there wasn't a formal job code or job description. This position was created to drive improved outcomes for our healthcare partners. There were a lot of "nay-sayers" very early on who did not believe in the role and my capabilities to make a difference. They didn't believe that a role within our organization could drive positive results for the health system. Contrarily, as a result of this position, programmatic rigor, and strong collaboration with various department leaders and nursing, the health system saw a significant increase in patient satisfaction.

Senior leaders within my organization began to take notice and realized that there were benefits to the Patient Experience Manager role. Five months post-graduation (Fall 2017), I was promoted into what the Regional executive leadership called a Regional Patient Experience Director. This position offered me the opportunity to work with healthcare partners throughout the East Coast to improve patient satisfaction. Now, it is important to mention that the title of this position remained informal. I was a director with an increased salary, yet the "official job description and title" did not exist. I waited patiently. I knew that a door would open, and I wanted to be the first person in our organization to "pioneer" a role that was once thought of as "ineffective" or "irrelevant" as an effective means to improve patient satisfaction. I was determined to remain humble, keep my head down, work hard, and keep the faith.

Sometimes our biggest blessings come when we are patient. I remained focused and closed my ears to negative commentary from individuals who did not want to see me succeed. After the implementation of the company's Patient Experience program, several of our healthcare system partners along the East Coast demonstrated significant patient satisfaction improvement. This was a WIN for me! And the organization, of course. The program worked, and I demonstrated the ability to lead this initiative for other health systems. Exactly one year later the company recognized my efforts. In December 2018, I was appointed to the role of National Patient Experience Director. It was official…job code and job description. I was patient, believed God, and it happened! This is an amazing opportunity, and it is even more extraordinary that I will be the FIRST individual to lead this initiative in the history of the organization...pioneer status.

Conclusion & Closing Thoughts

My doctoral degree and professional efforts have produced fruitful experiences. In October 2017, I was the recipient of the organization's highest award for frontline employees. It was a wonderful experience to share with my mother. We were invited to participate in a fun-filled, empowering week on a resort in Phoenix, Arizona with 200 other employees from across the world.

Community work is important. Growing up in the inner-city, there were times when my friends and I didn't have opportunities to attend extracurricular events. I believe these experiences have fueled a passion for helping and giving back to those in need. A few years ago, my organization, in partnership with the Urban League of Philadelphia (ULP), adopted a 9th grade class in one of Philadelphia's at-risk high schools. In November 2018, I was offered the opportunity to serve as an Executive Sponsor for a community pilot project in partnership with ULP. This initiative exposes and prepares high school students for college and for professions with my organization.

There are many obstacles that may come your way in the pursuit of your doctorate degree, and I would like to recommend several tips to keep in mind along the journey:

- First, you must identify "why" you decided to pursue your degree. It's your "why" that will motivate you to continue your journey. It is that same "why" that will facilitate the development of your dissertation topic. Understanding your "why" will help you to navigate hurdles and motivate you to move forward even when roadblocks present themselves.

- Second, I believe it is important to collaborate/partner with individuals who successfully defended their dissertation. These individuals can offer advice and recommendations to successfully complete coursework as well as how to prepare for the dissertation process.

- Third, never isolate yourself. Work in groups, set up consistent meetings with your professors and advisors. The worst thing that a doctoral student can do is to feel that things will just work themselves out. No, your time is important, and you are spending thousands of dollars that should not be wasted. Many anxieties can be resolved with collaborative study sessions and scheduled conversations with professors/advisors throughout the semester.

- As for post-doctoral studies and "work-life", I would recommend that you identify someone within your organization to mentor you in your career. Mentors/sponsors are critically important and have served me well in my professional pursuits.

Finally, BELIEVE in yourself and WORK HARD! One of the biggest failures we sometimes make: We do not have faith in our ability to achieve and overcome circumstances, especially when times are difficult. The doctoral program and career pursuits may present many challenges, but we must always remember that "anything worth having comes with hardship and trial".

It may come with adversarial circumstances, and it is within those trials and challenging times that we identify the strength, resilience, determination, and knowledge that lies within us. So no matter what comes your way...Never Give Up! TRUST in your ABILITY! You have what it takes to be SUCCESSFUL and WIN!

About Dr. Elizabeth Holder

As a National Patient Experience Director within Aramark's Healthcare and Hospitality sector, **Dr. Elizabeth Holder** has demonstrated proven ability to foster strong relationships with hospital executives, front line managers, and nursing leadership to drive patient satisfaction outcomes in hospitality services. With a passion for organizational development, she believes that her role as a system leader is to develop a service culture that demonstrates value and respect for all patients and families.

Dr. Holder received her Bachelors of Arts degree in Psychology from Arcadia University and a Masters of Arts from LaSalle University. In March 2017, she successfully defended her dissertation titled, *Career Entry, Retention, and Advancement Enablers and Barriers for Black Female Nurses: An Interpretive Study*, in Saint Joseph University's (SJU) Interdisciplinary Doctor of Education Program for Educational Leaders (IDEPEL). During her tenure as a System Patient Experience Manager, Dr. Holder developed an insatiable research interest to understand the role of facilitators and barriers in the career success of Black female nurses. A diverse healthcare workforce plays a vital role in the patient experience outcomes for patients, and Dr. Holder believes this research will offer higher education institutions and healthcare organizations recommendations to improve the retention and advancement of Black female nurses in the profession.

Dr. Holder has received a number of honors over the years. She graduated Magna Cum Laude from LaSalle University in Clinical Counseling Psychology, with a focus in Industrial/Organizational Psychology. Most recently, she was inducted into the College of Arts and Sciences (SJU) honor society for graduating in the top 5% of the graduating class, and the recipient of the Rashford Award for an outstanding dissertation for her Ed.D. thesis.

Dr. Holder currently serves as a member of Delta Sigma Theta Sorority, Inc., Co-Executive Sponsor for Aramark Ignite (a youth college and career readiness program), a member of Aramark's Women Business Resource Network (WBRN), an active member of Aramark Building Community, a Diversity, Respect, and Inclusion Facilitator (MLH), member of the Urban

League of Philadelphia, a graduate of Philadelphia's Urban Leadership Forum, and a board member for Together for West Philadelphia.

SOCIAL WORK & GOVERNMENT

Dr. Danielle Whylly

DR. PIA L. SCOTT

Dr. Danielle Whylly

I never lose. I either win or learn.~ Nelson Mandela

Winners Never Quit and Quitters Never Win
By: Dr. Danielle Sweat Whylly

Introduction

I AM… Dr. Danielle Sweat Whylly; an introduction that I *still* rarely ever speak comfortably. It's still an interesting accomplishment to me, although exactly how I made it through – fades in and out of so many of my abundant memories.

I AM… a native New Yorker, by way of the Bronx, Yonkers, Stone Mountain, Avondale Estates, Clarkston, Lithonia, Tallahassee, Tampa, Decatur, and Atlanta.

I AM… a proud "Angora" of Clarkston High School, a two-time Florida A&M University "Rattler," and distinguished "Black Panther" of the Whitney M. Young, Jr. School of Social Work at Clark Atlanta University. After having obtained a Bachelors in Psychology and Criminal Justice, Masters of Social Work in Community Development, and a Doctorate in Social Work Policy, Planning and Administration; *I AM… still just an around-the-way girl with too many dreams to share and too many bruises to bear.*

Personal Experiences

There is not a defining moment in my life that I can recall saying to myself: self, I want to be called "Doctor" one day. Each life experience has just propelled me forward – from one challenging moment to the next, for as long as I can remember. After each one, I would stop and think quietly: what's next, Danielle? I did know as a small child that I wanted to help people. I just didn't know how. As a young fair-skinned girl with hazel eyes, surrounded by beautiful browner-skinned family members who jokingly called me names like "White Folks," it became clear to me that skin color – not race – but skin tone would be a challenge for some reason. Coming of age around drugs, alcoholism, incarceration, cussing, fussing, fighting, and somewhat abusive ways of people showing, running from or returning to love, also helped me develop this "angry compassion" for people addicted to pain, poison, and/or prison. Even throughout a tumultuous high schooling experience, riddled with hilarious highs, fun, and lasting relationships; I can still remember crying every single night of my entire junior year. I think I was deathly afraid of the person I was becoming but did not know how to turn it around on my own. I was making so many poor decisions based on fleeting emotion – it's no wonder that anytime I pause to reflect, my eyes fill with tears at the very thought of just how far grace and mercy have carried me...from one challenging moment to the next. All in all – Florida A&M represented an opportunity to hit the reset button. Yet, while my collegiate matriculation was the absolute best to be had atop the 'highest of seven hills' at any HBCU there is – it still came with its fair share of growing pains. Despite seven car accidents, a month without lights and water, which included washing up before class at the Circle K, 9/11, break-ins, rooftop run-ins, and so much more – I still managed to graduate on time, and with all of my hair, teeth and toes intact. #wontHEdoit.

I didn't know any more about my direction until two very special people politely fell into my lap: Mrs. Perkins and Dr. Ola. They unknowingly flung me down the best path I would have never chosen for my own life, and I never turned back. *Along this unimaginable journey of substance and shame; with too many people to name and beautiful blessings to claim - I have no earthly idea exactly how I got over!*

Professional Experiences

On day one of my Masters of Social Work (MSW) program, Dr. Langley made one thing clear: we were now entering the "Black Educated Elite" and notwithstanding surmounting debt. And for those that planned to continue on to a doctoral program, especially the ladies; "don't think you'll find an equal amount of brothers on the same playing field as you." This was one harsh reality he made sure we understood before going any further. His words stuck with me and added to my already "angry compassion"-filled duffle bag. "Who cares," I thought. But for some, the look on their faces told it all! For me - I knew I was in the right space!

Surprisingly, my professional journey has been a much smoother ride than the personal one. Outside of my world of work beginning at age 14, each opportunity has worked in my favor, including the overnight security gig! I've met amazing people trekking through this life with as much uncertainty as I, unbothered by my goals and dreams, and unaware of the inner turmoil fueling them. See, I've never been one to talk much about what I plan to do, or what I am working on. But before you know it - *Voila!* One challenge down, the next one to go. If there's one consistent thing, Louise, Mary, Tito, and Gloria showed me how to do, is **KEEP IT MOVING**. No matter what you have to purge or pawn, you keep it moving; meanwhile, that duffle bag of "angry compassion" grows into a nice, neat suitcase…

One professional experience that always stood tall to me was my work as a young substance abuse counselor at a residential facility for teen boys. I learned so much about the addictions I already found familiar and even more about my own struggles. I learned to dodge chairs being hurled at me; not to ever sit with my back to the office door; and that letting go is a healthy pain when used appropriately. I truly enjoyed every opportunity I found myself in and appreciated every emotional lesson learned. Four years in, and I began practicing self-care about as regularly as brushing my teeth. One colleague quickly taught me, "When you're dead and gone, all they'll do is replace your name tag, girl." Likewise, I taught him my motto at the time, which was: "I'd rather have more memories than money," determined to do any and everything my 20s would allow. Most importantly, I was learning to care for myself along the way.

At some point, I remember deciding that I did want a doctorate degree. Not because my profession demanded one. But because I just wanted to see if I could do it. I wanted to research social issues that constantly gave me heartburn. I also liked the sound of publishing as "Dr. Somebody's Wife." I loved learning, and therefore had the thought of setting a new bar in my family, leaving a legacy that my siblings could strive for, and my cousins would be proud of. After all, who said that I couldn't? If I made it through some ump-teen-hundred other bumps and bruises, what could a couple more hurt? The concept of being "in school" for 25 years, including Head Start and Pre-K, only ever crossed my mind while trying to write papers at 3:27 a.m., on three hours of sleep with the help of coffee and No-Doze (DEFINITELY NOT RECOMMENDED)! Hell, I'd survived worse! And although professors insisted that pursuing the Ph.D. for some randomly abstract philosophical reason like mine would almost guarantee an abandoned motivation by Year 7 of "ABD" status (meaning All But Dissertation completed); I managed to press my way forward anyhow. I stumbled upon a program that despised standardized testing as much as I did AND specialized in culturally appropriate training. Then lo and behold; found myself interviewing with a stern and sassy Dr. Calloway of Clark Atlanta University inside of the Stonecrest Mall food court... and the rest is history.

Conclusion & Closing Thoughts

All in all, the pursuit of a terminal degree has taught me this: it gets lonely. Very, very lonely. There is no authentic way to adequately explain how something can feel so important to you, yet seem so boring and meaningless to everyone else outside of your program. When you hear someone say, "Wow, you're STILL in school?," it outweighs the 10 other people that have already said, "Girl, I'm so proud of you for going all the way!" So while good gospel music, tearful prayers, personal pity parties, self-encouragement, and an occasional afterthought of 'NOW - WHY AM I DOING THIS AGAIN?' became my closest friends; I also learned that loneliness does not mean alone. I also learned that treating myself to massages, a pair of nice shoes and ice cream every once in a while worked out just fine. Whatever it would take to cross that finish line. Little did I know that my King and Prince Charming, otherwise known as my husband and firstborn son, would be there waiting for their Doctor-Wifey-Mommy-around-the-way-girl-Social Worker, with open arms. Looking back I can honestly say that these two were *definitely* how I got over.

About Dr. Danielle S. Whylly

Dr. Danielle Sweat Whylly currently serves as the Community Outreach Specialist for the United States Attorney's Office for the Northern District of Georgia. In this capacity, she develops and fosters relationships between the U.S. Attorney's Office and the community by creating partnerships, prevention and ex-offender re-entry initiatives, and opportunities for staff to engage with residents throughout the District. In 2013 and 2017, Danielle received a U.S. Attorney's Award for her dedication and commitment to the pursuit of justice.

Over the past 15 years, she has proudly served in the well-rounded social work capacities of adolescent and women's substance abuse counseling, adolescent behavioral modification, cultural diversity, human trafficking and hate crime training and outreach, juvenile delinquency prevention, family advocacy, community development, policy research, and grant writing. Dr. Whylly is also a proud member of the Metro-Atlanta Professional Chapter of SISTUHS, Incorporated, author of Pillow Talk...sshhh! and co-author of bitter SWEET: A 52-Week Poetry Devotional.

A native New Yorker, Danielle is a graduate of Florida Agricultural and Mechanical University (FAMU), receiving both a Bachelor of Science degree in Psychology and a Master of Social Work degree in Administration and Community Development. Danielle earned her doctorate degree from Clark Atlanta University, in Social Work Policy, Planning, and Administration and currently resides in Metro-Atlanta with her husband and two children.

FINANCE

Dr. Jermani Thompson

Dr. Jermani Thompson

Research is formalized curiosity. It is poking and prying with a purpose.
—Zora Neale Hurston

Yet I Rose

By: Dr. Jermani Felicia Thompson

Introduction

Putting the experience of my doctoral journey in writing brings great joy and long overdue reflection. I learned as a young woman that an education would take me places the other women in my family had not dared or had the opportunities to ascend. Like a few other African-American women in my age group, I was the first of a dynamic matriarchal lineage to graduate from college. I did not grow up in a single parent home. I grew up in a home with a toxic environment.

Education, specifically reading and debate became my refuge to cope and escape. I successfully defended my doctoral work in 2016 and earned a Doctor of Philosophy degree in Industrial Organizational Psychology from the University of Phoenix. The discipline of Industrial Organizational Psychology affords me the opportunity to put analytical, process, and research skills into action each day. The primary decision to pursue a doctoral degree was rooted in my desire to teach, consult, and tell stories. I earned a Bachelor of Arts degree in English Literature and a special honors designation in African-American Studies from Mercer University in Macon, Georgia.

Personal Experiences: My Path to a Doctorate Degree Was Not a Straight Line

At a young age, I developed a love for words. Curious is one of the words repeatedly used to describe me. Reading fed by insatiable curiosity and fostered my use of words to express myself. Zora Neale Hurston immediately became my favorite author once I discovered her literary work in high school. Throughout primary and secondary school, I thought I wanted to be a corporate lawyer. My grandmother would joke that I could be a Philadelphia lawyer because I debated or questioned almost everyone and everything. Heaven help the person who tried to debate with me, and I knew I was right.

As I entered college, my plan was to major in political science and pursue a legal career working as a corporate lawyer. Counsel provided to me by a wise advisor redirected me to a degree in English. Her rationale was that English would be needed to pass the written portion of the LSAT. A strong writing acumen would also be needed to write a deposition or a legal brief. She also schooled me on how the law worked. Law books were in the library, and the content rarely changed. Being the logical person I am, I agreed with her assessment. I decided to major in English. I do not regret the decision. However, I do regret not taking one additional class to earn a minor in Sociology.

Leading up to the conclusion of my first year of college, I attended a job fair and landed a job with a major bank. I was hired as a summer travel teller. The expectation was to work during the summer to fill in for tellers who were on vacation. As an African-American female, I heard and took to heart a very common message repeated to us – you have to be twice as good to get half as far. Because of the work ethic and message to be twice as good, I was asked to remain on the active payroll and work during holidays or whenever I was in town for long weekends.

Because I went to school less than two hours away from home and the region I would be working in, the offer was enticing. I accepted the offer without hesitation. As a broke college student, the extra cash and work experience appealed to my workaholic and perfectionist sensibilities. After the first summer, I worked every summer, holiday, and long weekend until I graduated from college.

After graduating from college, I moved back to Atlanta although my immediate family had moved to Jacksonville, Florida. I returned to the bank as a summer travel team teller. My plan was to work for a year to save money and study for the LSAT. A management training program leader I had worked for was managing one of the locations I was assigned to the summer after I graduated. He and I connected professionally because we both had an interest in law. We joked that working for a bank required us to know so many laws and regulations; we were getting hands-on experience. He was a rising star in the Atlanta market. He invited me to join his team as a full-time employee. Again as a practical person, I assumed being a teller and working "banker's hours" still allowed me time to study for the LSAT and make money.

Little did I know that he wanted me to be a Teller Manager, which was a new role created to manage all Tellers and the operations of the retail center. Although I enjoyed helping people, I had no desire to manage people. He believed in me, and I am an overachiever. I accepted the job. I progressed quickly up the corporate ladder within the bank, and the salary kept rising as well. Studying and taking the LSAT was quickly in the rearview mirror of my life after two years. The summer and holiday job was my entry point into an over 20-year career in the financial services industry as well as the first detour on my doctoral journey.

Professional Experiences: The Professed Corporate Lawyer Becomes a Banker

Although I could not name it in my early twenties, I discovered a passion to help others. Instead of pursuing a career in the legal field, I gravitated toward Human Resources. Being a spiritual person, I knew I had the gifts of help and discernment. After becoming a manager, the skills that quickly came to the forefront as strengths were coaching, mentoring, and teaching. As an intellectually curious learner, I knew I wanted to go back to school and earn an advanced degree.

However, after two years of working, winning awards, and getting consistent raises; being a lawyer was no longer a desire. The manager who gave me my start as a manager, was also being promoted. He had promoted and rewarded me. When he left, I was the assistant manager. The new manager arrived, and we established a great rapport. She was in the management training program, and she nominated me for the program. Even though I did not want to go to law school, I also knew I did not want to manage a retail banking center. At that time, the bank had a Human Resource (HR)Generalists who supported the banks.

The HR Generalist who supported the center where I worked suggested a path in HR for me. Being the curious researcher I began looking into HR degrees. Georgia State University offered master's degree programs in Public Administration with a concentration in HR Personnel Management and another program in heritage preservation. I applied to the Heritage Preservation program and was denied.

Looking back, I believe my application to the Heritage Preservation program was a form of self-sabotage. I had no idea what I wanted to do with the degree if I had earned it. I applied and was admitted into the Master of Public Administration program at Georgia State University. I worked during the day and earned a Master's of Public Administration degree in 1999. Yes, I continued to work full time and went to school full time to finish the program in 18 months. Between 1998 and 1999 I was so driven, I did not recognize the negative perception I was displaying to family, friends, and coworkers.

The most adverse impact was on my coworkers. My driven personality, need for perfectionism, and ambition was coming across in different ways to different employees in the bank. The team I worked with day-to-day viewed me as tough, inflexible, ambitious, and unapproachable. Regional and state leaders perceived me as a great operational leader who could get the work done, manage the risks, reduce losses, and keep the customers happy. I was the go-to person to send to failing centers and get it in shape. While the money, rewards, and accolades rolled in from senior leaders; I did not have a rapport with the teams who reported to me. The relationships were purely transactional. Enter detour number two.

Personal Experiences: Time to Switch Things Up

The concentration of my MPA was Human Resources Management. I thought my dream job was an HR Director by way of an HR Generalist, Talent Acquisition Manager, and Training Delivery Manager. Clearly, I was a planner. As I was entering my final semester of graduate school, the company I worked for moved from having local HR Generalists to a centralized call center model. After visiting Charlotte in early 1999, I knew I did not want to move to the city. In my mind, I had accomplished the task in the retail banking space in Atlanta. I opted to move to Jacksonville, FL to manage a call center team. At least in Jacksonville, I had family.

I graduated from Georgia State University on a Saturday, moved to Jacksonville the next day (Sunday), and began work the following day (Monday). Did I mention I was an ambitious overachiever? I was always perceived by classmates and coworkers as an overachiever, extremely smart, and not a people person. The perception was not far off from reality. Honestly, the perception was 100% accurate. I am an introvert, and the perception of being unapproachable is something I had to work hard to mask as a manager of people.

The call center team I was assigned to manage was responsible for second tier support. I arrived in Jacksonville in August 1999. By 2001, I had worked my way up to the number one call center manager in the company. I was rewarded with a trip to Maui, Hawaii. Upon my return from Maui, my ambition to do more, be more, learn more, called to my inner being.

I desired to move into a traditional Human Resources role because I still had a goal to be an HR professional. On the way up the ladder in Jacksonville, FL, I met my former husband and transitioned into a training and development job. Two pivotal experiences changed my need for perfectionism and redirected my professional drive. The first was the attack on the New York twin towers in 2001, commonly known as 9/11. I was the senior trainer in the office that day. I remember getting a call from my then fiancé stating that the naval base he worked on was on lockdown and to turn on the news. I was responsible for the disaster recovery activities in the training facility. I went to both training classes to deliver the news.

The second pivotal moment was my marriage in 2002. I became a Navy wife and my husband received orders to go overseas to Bahrain for an unaccompanied tour of duty. I was married and living alone. A longing for a doctoral degree rose back up during 2002 and 2003, and then the training and development job led to a job as an Anti-Money Laundering Compliance Specialist. My curiosity and corporate climb began anew. The corporate climb was in full throttle until I had my son in 2005. I continued to work, hold down a household, and mother a beautiful baby boy until I hit a wall in 2006 when my husband and I moved to Atlanta. This was detour number three.

Conclusions & Closing Thoughts

After moving back to Atlanta, I realized I could no longer sustain a workaholic and perfectionist mentality. I also realized I was not able to have everything I wanted the way I wanted and remain true to myself. In retrospect, I gave up and gave away some of my personality and self-esteem during my first marriage to appease and serve someone who was not reciprocating where and when needed. My son is the best gift from my first marriage. I still have the son, not the husband. I am grateful for the lessons learned from the first marriage. We separated in 2009 and divorced in 2010.

I learned what I need in a partner, lover, and companion through much self-reflection and therapy. I mustered the courage to make known I was no longer happy with the organization I worked for, but did not quit. I did become disengaged from the work. I left the company in 2011. I went through a grieving period but was relieved that I was not bound to a job that longer served my needs. I was free to follow my heart and passion. I enrolled in the University of Phoenix School of Advanced Studies Industrial Organizational Psychology program and began classes August 2012.

The journey to a doctorate was not easy. It was also not a J.D., but a Ph.D. The nine-month pause during the doctoral program, the epiphany I had while curled up in the fetal position on the floor of a bathroom during a break while attending residency in Phoenix, and waiting over a year between completing the degree and walking across the stage were worth it. I admit I am a recovering workaholic and perfectionist.

The inclusion of my chapter in this book is another step along my teaching journey. I am honored and humbled by the opportunity to share a few of my experiences as a tool of encouragement or confirmation for women who are on their own professional and educational journeys. My recommendation for any woman considering or going through the doctoral journey is threefold. First, know thyself. Understand and stand by what you like, dislike, love, can take, cannot take, and what passions drive you to power. The power of the internal fortitude will sustain you when you are in tears and feel like giving up – yes you will feel like giving up.

Secondly, establish a strong and praying "village" to fortify you from the outside when you through the tough times. There will be tough times – mental, physical, financial, emotional and a few other adjectives mixed in along the way. The village should consist of loving family members and friends who will push, pull, and applaud you through every milestone. I am eternally grateful for your tough love, support, prodding, and cheers on this journey.

Finally, select a topic that excites you turns you on, and that you are willing to live with (literally and figuratively) for the rest of time. A dissertation topic becomes an appendage of you. Do not fall into the myth that you must publish or perish or do something magnificent in someone else's eyes. Doctoral research should be personal. After knowing who you are, establishing the village, and selecting an area of research, choose a committee who will complement your journey, not dictate your journey. The twists, turns, tears, and feelings of hopelessness will come. Press on. Perseverance is the key.

This chapter is dedicated to my bright, handsome, and patient son who accompanied me on many library visits and proofread a few chapters of my dissertation. I also dedicate these thoughts as reflection and gratitude to the memory of the matriarchs of my family whose spirits carried me when I wanted to give up. They are my grandmother (Janie Mae) and aunt (Ruby Madelyn) who were here to celebrate every degree before this one and are smiling down because we now have a doctor in the family. Although my doctoral journey is complete, I still have many miles to travel. I am now formalizing my curiosity by poking and prying with a purpose.

About Dr. Jermani Thompson

Dr. Jermani "Felicia" Thompson is the founder and principal consultant of JSquared Management Consulting. She is a native of Atlanta who brings over 20 years of experience in the financial services industry as a senior leader in various roles within Human Resources, Anti-Money Laundering Compliance, Quality & Productivity, and Retail Banking. After graduating in the top 10% of the charter class of Lovejoy High School, Dr. Jermani pursued and earned a Bachelor of Arts Degree in English from Mercer University and a Master of Public Administration degree with a concentration in Human Resource Personnel Management from Georgia State University Andrew Young School of Policy Studies.

After earning her Ph.D. in Industrial Organizational Psychology from the University of Phoenix, Dr. Jermani launched JSquared to help businesses and individuals unleash the power behind their passion through exponential coaching, by making connections and promoting constructive collaboration. In addition to assisting emerging and established leaders discover the power behind their passion, Dr. Jermani chases her passion for words by writing journal articles and speaking about women's leadership at national and international conferences.

Although Dr. Jermani has lived in two other states, she is a Georgia peach to the core and always finds herself on a midnight train or red-eye to Georgia. She is active in multiple nonprofit organizations as a volunteer and board member. She is also a member of the Gwinnett County Chapter of Delta Sigma Theta Sorority, Inc. Dr. Jermani currently resides in Northern Metro Atlanta with her son, Justyn.

EDUCATION & COUNSELING

Dr. Kennedi Dixon
Dr. Latinia Shell

Dr. Kennedi Dixon

The race is not to the swift but to those who endureth to the end.
~Ecclesiastes 9:11 and Hebrews 3:14

Denial Does Not Mean Defeat: Determination Finishes the Course

By: Dr. Kennedi Strickland-Dixon

Introduction

As a first-generation college student from a single parent home, I am beyond grateful to be a part of this project. I'm honored to share my educational journey and the experiences of my 24 years in the field of special education. In 2013, I received a doctorate in Educational Leadership from DePaul University in Chicago, Illinois and was thereby endorsed to be a superintendent.

When asked to include a favorite quote in this chapter, I immediately thought of one that combines two passages from Ecclesiastes and Hebrews, and as it says, slow and steady effort wins the race. In my role as a Director of Special Education, I understand that my purpose in life is to give voice to a population of students who are often voiceless; my journey in education was not my choice alone, but truly God's intended plan. It is my hope that this project will speak for those who feel alone and encourage them to finish the course.

Personal Experiences: My Induction into Education and Newly Defined Friendships

The spark that lights a burning desire to pursue a doctorate is different for each person. In my case, someone planted an important seed in me at a time in my life when I most needed mentorship. My road to obtaining a doctorate began while attending my local community college immediately after high school. During my time at Triton College from 1990-92, I met two African-American individuals who truly changed my life. Dr. Thomas had recently completed his doctorate, and Dr. Moore was completing hers as well. This was the first time someone had a conversation with me about pursuing a doctorate; I had no clue what it meant or what was needed to obtain it. As a teenager, I had no idea how immeasurably their countless conversations would affect my life.

During these conversations, Dr. Thomas encouraged me to pursue a bachelor's degree in special education. He told me I had to go for the doctoral degree because that was the only way to secure a seat at the table. Dr. Moore was writing her dissertation about women at community colleges and their contributions in leadership. From these conversations, I learned that Black women didn't have a role in conversations about education other than that of a traditional school teacher. I understood that the pursuit of a doctorate was necessary for a Black woman in the field of education, and my determination to have a role in the conversations became the fuel that propelled me toward my goal.

The real purpose of the doctorate would come to me later, during the years I spent in the field in the low-income school district where I received my earliest formal education: my elementary school experience was another foundation of purpose for me. As a child, during my K-8 experience, I encountered Black men and women who ensured we emerged proud of our culture and with an understanding that we were smart and that nobody could take that away from us. The White teachers knew the expectations of the school and held students to that level of excellence. A sense of community existed in the neighborhood. My mother was the only single mother on the block and was just as involved in the school as the other mothers. I knew we struggled, but I had no concept of what it truly meant to be poor because my teachers had spoken so much life into me that I didn't feel any different from anyone else.

When I completed college and took my first teaching position in what had been home to me, the feel of the community had changed. All of the teachers were now White and the racial lines that divided the neighborhoods of the district were now clear to me. The disparities that existed in special education were also clear. Special education was often an afterthought, a separate entity that existed parallel to the "real" work that went on in the building. I now understood what Dr. Thomas meant about having a seat the table. I was not in a position to make any decisions beyond my classroom. At the suggestion of some seasoned Black teachers in my building, I began a master's program that led to my first supervisory role in special education. This road outside of the classroom led to me becoming the first African-American Director of Special Education from 2004-12; I am still the only African-American to have held that position in the district.

As the Director, I had that seat at the table that empowered me to make decisions for special education students and my decisions made it clear that students of color were meaningful and not to be taken lightly. I was able to work diligently with the staff to eradicate very antiquated practices and move the district forward; ensuring special education was no longer an afterthought in planning or practice. I had the good fortune of serving under an African-American female superintendent from the neighborhood who was working on a doctorate. The reason and purpose of the doctorate began to intersect. Dr. Richardson-Broughton took me under her wing and helped me to understand that the real seat of impact rested within the superintendent's office. The beliefs of a superintendent are embedded in the beliefs of a school. In order to make the greatest impact and become a change agent for impoverished students, I had to seek the superintendent's seat.

I chose DePaul University for its history of being grounded in social justice. DePaul University utilizes an Urban Teaching Framework that examines the impact of race in education, particularly in low–income areas heavily populated with students of color. For me, DePaul made sense of all of the emotions, beliefs, and goals I wanted to achieve in my role as an educator. Having completed my first three degrees at a predominately White institution, I wanted a different experience that would be meaningful for students of color.

The doctoral experience has truly impacted my personal relationships with family, friends, church members, and my Delta Sorority Sisters. Of the all the lessons and advice that can be given about this process of obtaining a Ph.D., a critical observation that cannot be underestimated concerns the demise of existing relationships and building of new relationships. This process can stress marriages and relationships a great deal. There are many emotions that will come along, and you will need to be centered with someone who will let you melt down and yet offer you a strong hand to help rebuild your stamina, self-esteem, and self-worth. The support of family and friends will be critical. My husband was and still is my constant calm in the midst of every personal and professional storm I experience.

When I began the doctoral program, my boys were six and two years old—I know, what was I thinking! My husband held down our household on so many levels I cannot detail in this short chapter. My family, church family, and friends stepped in and helped with our children. Be advised that this process will reveal who your "real" friends are. It is critical to note that not everyone will be happy for you and may be quietly hoping that you are not successful in obtaining your educational desires. I am tremendously blessed to have a Sister Circle that has been my "Ride or Die" since elementary and high school. My Sister Circle encouraged me, prayed for me, and continues to celebrate me because they know that this journey has been far from easy. There were many events with family, friends, and Sorors that I was unable to attend. You will have to learn not to beat yourself up about your absences that are due to the tasks and commitments necessary to complete the journey. My attendance and involvement in church was something that was non-negotiable for me and my family because I needed that spiritual refueling and the prayers of my church family to help sustain me during my darkest days.

It is critically important that you establish a small group of people in your program to start and end the writing process with. This relationship will be critical in determining your success or failure. When you are in your coursework, you are on someone else's time. When the coursework ends, you have to have the discipline to write. Having the discipline to write will prove to be your greatest challenge. My writing group consisted of two other African-American ladies. For two years, we met twice a month. We set timelines, adhered to the timelines we established and held each other accountable. During this time, each of us experienced a personal tragedy that affected our motivation to finish. We cried together, laughed together, accepted no excuses from each other, and ultimately, walked the stage together as Dr. Coleman, Dr. Hill, and Dr. Dixon. These sisters are so important in my life and were truly necessary for my completion of the program.

The love I receive from my community and classmates regarding the completion of the doctorate and my professional accomplishments truly me humble on so many levels because the pride they have in me is genuine. My greatest challenges has been with folks from the neighborhood who believed I have suddenly changed and now expect to be called Dr. Kennedi Dixon when nothing could be further from the truth. Initially, I found myself feeling very defensive and wanting to show people I am still just Suki from the neighborhood. No titles needed. I have used my nickname in the community since birth and continue to do so. I reserve Dr. Dixon for professional purposes only. Remain grounded in who you were prior to completing your doctorate is critically important so that you do not become caught up in being defined by a title. Most important is the person behind the title and how you use the title to impact the lives of others.

Professional Experiences: The Journey to Completion

At the onset of pursuing my doctoral degree, I was in the district in which I was born and raised. I had the pleasure of establishing myself as a committed leader with a proven track record for bringing about positive outcomes for kids and families. My staff and co-workers celebrated me every step of the way and encouraged me when I most needed encouragement. As the old saying goes, everything that glitters ain't gold. There were some White co-workers at the Central Office and select school board members who didn't want me to finish and took every opportunity to remind me that my White counterparts had finished ahead of me. Some people who finished before me also seemed to try to sow the seeds of doubt. It is important to recognize these distractions for what they are and move forward.

During the dissertation process, I left the district that was home to me. Many perceived this move as something that would prove detrimental to my writing process and urged me to stay until the writing was completed. I am taking a pause to elaborate on the importance of this professional move. As a part of God's plan, my new superintendent, Dr. Murphy, welcomed me, celebrated me, and strongly encouraged me to finish strong. There will be things that will come along in the workplace that will add levels of stress. It is important that you do not let these things overwhelm you or deter you from completing the process. You must have a laser focus on completion, regardless of the cost or persecution associated with finishing.

Currently, I work in an affluent school district that is culturally diverse in its student population but lacks diversity in its faculty. In many respects, I have felt that transitioning into my current position with my level of education has proven to be both an asset and an obstacle. Given the school's history of academic excellence and accolades, it is considered a very difficult institution to serve as a faculty member without being highly qualified and decorated with honors; however, I have encountered many instances in which the doctor in my professional title has not been respected or well- received. Interestingly, Black members of the organization who are not faculty but are employed in other areas genuinely extend a great deal of respect towards me. These individuals remind me why the title of doctor is so important to impacting students of color at my school. I overcome these obstacles daily by focusing on the needs of the kids I serve. What I love the most about my job is that the needs of special education students transcend color. The kids give me life and help me remain focused on God's intended purpose for me: to serve those without a voice. I constantly remind myself that I am a servant to the voiceless, not a servant to people with power or prestige.

Conclusion and Closing Thoughts

I titled my contribution to this work "Denial Does Not Mean Defeat" for many personal reasons. My journey to completion was extremely difficult for many reasons. The greatest challenge was my first committee. The first committee consisted of three middle-aged White women who felt threatened by a dissertation that focused on the impact of race on the historically marginalized. My first committee didn't read my work, offered no suggestions for literature, and ultimately wasted a year and a half of my time. I watched as other members of my class finished and moved on with their lives. I felt stuck, all alone, and discouraged to the point of giving up. I am grateful for the mentorship of Dr. Stovall and Dr. Lewis. They encouraged me to keep writing regardless of the efforts of my committee. This proved to be the best advice in ensuring I finished the process. Remember: Never stop writing regardless of how discouraged you may feel. Continue to stay grounded in the research and keep current your annotations and works cited.

After a year and a half, I dismissed my committee, secured a new Chair (Dr. Hall), and invited Dr. Lewis onto my committee. Dr. Hall gave me new life and patiently worked through my feelings of doubt, defeat, and distrust. He added a White female professor to my committee who did peer reviews for scholarly journals. Her final thoughts in her critique of my dissertation was that it read like a book and was extremely well written; as she stated, this was a challenge for many doctoral students. I highlighted this experience to share with readers a testimony about having confidence in yourself when you may not feel supported by professors. Though my previous committee questioned the scholarly merit of my topic and tried to convince me that my writing style was difficult to follow, I remained true to my commitment of sharing the resilient narratives of Black males who overcame the stigma and disparity associated with special education and successfully attended college. I am sharing this section to discourage your spirit of doubt and to replace it with determination to finish the course.

I would alert Black women that the doctoral process can be very dark without a support system if you are not surrounded by others on the same journey. I would highly encourage you to pick a topic that you have a great deal of interest. Given the fact that you will need to eat, sleep, and drink your dissertation topic, it must be near and dear to your being. It is critical to set and execute goals and imperative that you set nonnegotiable timelines in order to succeed. Be sure to take the time to unwind, whether that's with a lunch date for one, a massage, or just some quiet time.

I would be remiss if I didn't use this opportunity to encourage Black women in the doctoral process to focus on topics about Black people. Absent from dissertations are stories about us and by us. If we are not writing narratives about ourselves, who will?

My dissertation was the springboard for me to begin to present at professional conferences and to gain consulting jobs with school districts. My work has been well received at professional conferences. As I work on this chapter, I am simultaneously preparing professional presentations about developing and sustaining culturally relevant IEP meetings for families of color and about the impact of teacher relationships on the success or failure of students of color. I have had the opportunity to guest lecture and will be seeking adjunct work in addition to my position in the public school setting. None of this work would have been possible without first obtaining my doctorate in Educational Leadership, and without my seat at the table, I never would have been in the position to help so many special education students.

About Dr. Kennedi Dixon

Dr. Kennedi Strickland-Dixon is currently the Special Education Divisional Director at Oak Park and River Forest High School. Prior to transitioning to Oak Park and River Forest High School, she served as the first African- American Director of Special Education at Maywood District 89 for eight years and the Director of Special Education and Student Services at Bellwood at Bellwood District 88.

In addition to her current position as a Special Education Director, Dr. Strickland- Dixon is heavily involved in promoting professional development that explores the needs of African-American students in the educational setting. She has presented at several professional conferences and is a guest lecturer at DePaul University the institution in which she received her doctorate in Educational Leadership. She is on the Board of Directors for the Mary E. Smith Foundation, which works to advance brain tumor research.

Dr. Strickland- Dixon is a member of Delta Sigma Theta Sorority, Incorporated. Dr. Strickland-Dixon is actively involved in her church Garden of Prayer MB Church. Despite her tremendously busy schedule, her greatest accomplishments rest with her husband of 21 years Christopher Dixon, Sr. and her two teenage boys Christopher, Jr. and Kyle.

Dr. Latinia Shell

We are because I am, and because I am, therefore, We Are. ~John Mbiti

From the Projects to the Professoriate: Wouldn't take anything from my Journey to discovering my Purpose

By: **Dr. Latinia M. Shell, Ed.D., LPC, NCC, CCMHC, ACS**

Introduction

In this thing called life, we are all here on planet earth for a certain time period unbeknownst to us. In our lifetime, we are socialized to be reared and nurtured by our families, attend grade school to be educated, while learning the skills necessary to be prepared for the workforce. Once we graduate, we have different paths that we can take. Some pursue further education and/or training, and some go straight to the workforce. We are then socialized to start a career that will support our lifestyle, start a family (i.e., marriage, children, etc.), purchase or rent a home, and be productive citizens in society (i.e., community organizations, volunteerism, voting, etc.). However, depending on the amount of privilege that one has living here in America (i.e., race, gender, socio-economic status, etc.), the playing field may not be leveled, and the journey may be much more difficult for some. The purpose of this anthology is to share my personal and professional journey as a Black woman navigating this thing called life in the search for my purpose.

My name is Dr. Latinia M. Shell. My favorite quote is a combination of two African Proverbs: The first—"Each One, Reach One, Teach One"—originated during slavery when slaves/Africans were denied the right to become educated. If slaves were taught or self-taught how to read and write, it was their moral obligation to teach another slave/African how to read and write. The second—"We are because I am, and because I am, therefore, We are " by Kenyan-born, Christian, religious philosopher, and writer, John Mbiti—reflects on the importance of the collective group. Both quotes are symbolic of the importance and need to give back to the community.

As stated in Luke 12:48, "…For unto whomsoever much is given, much will be required …" (King James Version). With great power, comes great responsibility. I have been blessed to earn a Doctorate Degree in

Counseling Psychology in the field of Counseling. I am even more blessed to be able to share my gifts and talents with the numerous students and clients who I am very fortunate to work with.

Personal Experiences

My mother, who was a single parent, raised me. As a child, I remember how difficult it was for my mother trying to raise me by herself, going from job to job, having limited finances, and having to rely on welfare to pay bills and put food on the table. Due to my mother's financial circumstances, she qualified for public housing, and I grew up in the projects my entire childhood and we've even lived in several homeless shelters. With that said, I am grateful for my mother who showed me what struggle and sacrifice looked like first-hand, as well as the importance of education. I never allowed my socioeconomic status to hold me back. Instead, I used it as my fuel and motivation to end the cycle of poverty and to make something out of myself through education and hard work.

Education has definitely been the key to unlocking the door to fulfilling a successful future. I was first introduced to the notion of college in junior high school by my former Principal, Mr. Glover, who created a college-going culture for the entire student body and introduced me to my first college visit. From that moment on, I knew that I was going to college. It was my ticket out of extreme poverty.

In high school, I was so inspired by my former School Counselor, Mr. Hopkins, and his generosity and assistance in helping me to navigate the college process, which I decided to pursue a career as a School Counselor. Fortunately, I excelled in high school and was given a full minority academic scholarship to attend Millersville University as a first-generation college student, where I earned my BA in Psychology. I also received a Graduate Assistantship to continue my studies at Millersville University to pursue my Master's Degree in Counselor Education with a certification in Secondary School Counseling. While at Millersville University, I was inspired by my Undergraduate Professor, Dr. Smith Wade-El, and my Graduate Professor, Dr. Meyer, to pursue my Doctorate Degree in Counseling Psychology, so that I could teach in academia. After graduating with my Master's Degree, I obtained a full-time position as a School Counselor.

Simultaneously, I enrolled at Argosy University, Sarasota Campus' blended Doctoral Program. This was a turning point for me, as I was in my early 20s, experiencing being married, having a child, and becoming a mother (to both my son and 10-year-old nephew that my husband and I inherited and ended up raising); and trying to balance working full-time with being a part-time Doctoral Student. Needless to say, this impacted my personal relationships immensely. Many of my colleagues that I started the Doctoral Program with dropped out along the way due to life's circumstances, failing comps, getting divorced, etc. Fortunately for me, my strong connection to God, supportive husband and family, self-care, and strong connection and support from my cohort sustained me as a doctoral student and ultimately assisted me in being able to successfully defend my dissertation and fulfill requirements for graduation.

Professional Experiences

My professional journey spans over 20 years and various settings in schools, community, and academia. My first professional career was as a School Counselor for 10 years. At one school district, I was the only African American Faculty in the entire district that I worked in. In another district, I was the only African American School Counselor that I worked in. In all the school districts that I worked in, I was the only School Counselor pursuing a Doctoral Degree, as well as National Certification and Licensure. I always felt different from my colleagues. While most of my School Counselor Colleagues remained in their positions until retirement, I knew that School Counseling was just the beginning of my professional journey. It took me 7 years to earn my Doctorate Degree as a part-time student while working full-time.

Immediately, I was offered a position as a full-time, tenured, track-position member in a graduate program, where I was the only full-time African American Faculty member in the entire college. This was my ultimate dream job. Unfortunately, I soon realized that teaching online was not fulfilling for me. I applied to another institution where I could experience teaching face-to-face and got the position. At this university, I was the only full-time Faculty in the entire Graduate School and Counseling Program. Unfortunately, I was the subject of extreme bullying, discrimination, and a hostile work environment by the Chair of the Department. By my choice, I resigned.

Although I was deeply saddened and distraught, I soon realized that the experience was another turning point and launched me into my destiny. I was able to fulfill a dream in establishing my own Counseling Private Practice. I am proud to say that I have been in Private Practice for the last 5 years. To date, I am one of the only African American, female, Private-Practice Entrepreneurs in the City of Lancaster. This year, I experienced another turning point as I was offered a full-time position as the Assistant Director of a Graduate Counseling Program at Missio Seminary, where I also teach graduate counseling courses. I feel so blessed that I am back in academia doing what I love—teaching graduate counseling students. Finally, I feel like I have the best of both worlds working in my private practice as a clinician, and working in academia as an Administrator and Professor!

Conclusions & Closing Thoughts

As I reflect upon my own credentials—Doctorate Degree in Counseling Psychology, License as a Professional Counselor, Certification as a National Certified Counselor, Clinical Mental Health Counselor, and Approved Counselor Supervisor; and accomplishments—Best of 2018 and 2017 Hall of Fame Lancaster Award for Private Practice, Minority Business Award for Private Practice, American Mental Health Counselors Association Research Award Winner for my Dissertation, Outstanding Entrepreneurial Service and Lasting Contribution for Civic Engagement Award from the NAACP for my Private Practice, and Steinman Fellowship Award for my Dissertation Research—all I can say is that I am truly blessed! God has blessed me with 20 years in the counseling profession—10 years as a School Counselor, 5 years in Private Practice, and over five years in academia both as an Adjunct and Full-Time Professor.

In conclusion, I'd like to offer some words of encouragement to my Black sisters and sisters in general who are both still in their Doctoral Programs, as well as those who have graduated and are working in their respective professions.

First of all, never give up! There will be times when you want to throw in the towel. When you are in the storm, know that if you keep pushing, you will end up on the other side, where your rainbow and pot of gold will be waiting. During the storm, keep your eye on the prize, keep your head up, and keep pushing. Also, seek support from a power higher than oneself (i.e., God, belief in a higher power, spirituality, etc.). It is during the storm that you may need to be carried along.

Second, have a supportive network of colleagues, friends, and family, as you will need to enlist support from all of them. Make time for self-care, and reward yourself when you accomplish short-term and long-term goals (i.e., scheduling massages, hair and nail spa pampering, exercise; eating healthy; sleeping; shopping; participating in a girls' night out; etc.). "Self-care is not about being selfish; it's about being self-full" as stated by the renowned author, speaker, and television host of Iyanla: Fix My Life, on OWN, Iyanla Vanzant. Also, make time for family. So much of your time is spent studying and working, and family could feel neglected, so make sure to schedule in family time to keep things balanced.

In addition, connect with other women who can offer support as mentors. Mentors are able to offer support, uplift, and empower mentees. As we experience success and accomplish our goals, we must not forget to reach back and help other Black sisters and sisters in general in reaching their goals.

Lastly, as stated by the late acclaimed American poet, storyteller, activist, and autobiographer, Dr. Maya Angelou, "I wouldn't take nothing for my journey now," and I am continuously striving to reach the goal.

About Dr. Latinia M. Shell

Dr. Latinia Shell is from Lancaster, PA. She is the Owner and CEO of Diversity Works, LLC, which is a Group Private Practice in the City of Lancaster, PA. In addition, Dr. Shell is the Assistant Director of the Graduate Counseling Program at Biblical Theological Seminary.

Dr. Shell received a Bachelor's Degree in Psychology and a Master's Degree in Counselor Education from Millersville University. She earned her Doctoral Degree in Counseling Psychology from Argosy University. She is a Licensed Professional Counselor in the State of PA, National Certified Counselor, Certified Clinical Mental Health Counselor, and Approved Clinical Supervisor.

Dr. Shell's experiences include 20 years of both teaching and counseling in school, college, community/mental health, and private practice settings. Her research area of interests includes racial identity development, multicultural counseling and cultural competence, social and racial justice, diversity inclusion in schools and in the workplace, supervision, and training, and self-care and wellness.

Dr. Shell enjoys spending time with her husband and son, traveling, playing tennis, reading, and listening to music.

DOCTORAL CANDIDATES

Janeé Stevenson

Tiffany Brannon

Janeé Stevenson

"Racial oppression is a traumatic form of interpersonal violence, which can lacerate the spirit, scar the soul, and puncture the psyche. Without a clear and descriptive language to describe this experience, those who suffer cannot coherently convey their pain, let alone heal." ~Dr. Kenneth V. Hardy

I Am Not Who They Say I Am, I Am More!
Janeé Stevenson M.Ed., M.A., M.S.

Introduction

There are not many platforms for Black women to share their experiences especially as it relates to pursuing a doctorate. I am ecstatic about the opportunity to join other professional Black women to tell "our story." I have spent over 19 years in the mental health field working with children, adolescents, and adults. Working in the field is rewarding, but it comes with its fair share of frustrations, which can result in burnout and feelings of helplessness. Dr. Hardy's quote resonates with me because I have often observed how trauma impacts and shapes how people perceive the world and their sense of self. To date, my life's work has been to help clients process their experiences and support them as they courageously seek healing. I am currently pursuing a doctorate degree in Clinical Psychology with an intended conferral date of August 2019. I am completing an internship at the University of Houston's Counseling and Psychological Services Center, as a final requirement of my Doctor of Psychology (Psy.D) degree. My hope in participating in this book project is to encourage and empower other Black women to never give up. It is inevitable that barriers will manifest, failures will occur, but we come from a lineage of people who have endured many hardships, many trials but have ultimately proven, *I Am Not Who They Say I Am, I Am More!*

Personal Experiences

I never imagined that I would be able to say that I am close to finishing my doctorate degree in a Clinical Psychology program at the age of 42 while being a wife and mother of four. After all, according to societal expectations of me as an African American female born in Camden, NJ, raised in an underserved community in Philadelphia, PA, the product of public school education and born to parents who were not college educated, I should not be here. So, I am what some would consider an anomaly. And I must admit, it is difficult to see your true potential when others are defining it for you, but despite many obstacles, successes, and failures, I am proud to be a role model for the next generation of "anomalies."

In high school, I was lucky to have Black male and female mentors who were instrumental in teaching the importance of getting an education and holding me accountable when I fell short of maximizing my academic potential. I also experienced the same level of support from Black professors in my undergraduate program. My mentors were great role models and were quickly able to identify my greatness even when I was unsure. My parents and grandparents were great sources of support. None of them attended college but made it clear that they wanted better for me thus, sacrificing immensely to put me through college. In recognizing the mentorship I received and honoring the sacrifices of my parents, I understood that I had to make them proud and that failure was not an option.

Deciding to pursue a doctoral degree later in life, while married with children, definitely takes a toll on your marriage and impacts the lives of your children. When I began my program, my children's ages were 16, 11, 8, and 5 and I had been married for 12 years. I was working full time and determined to fight through any obstacle. I was optimistic and energetic about taking on such a tall task; however, I quickly realized the difficulty in managing it all. The excellence that embodies the Black woman, like the ability to be resilient, persistent, assertive, a multi-tasker, and caretaker of her family, is also what propels us to succeed amid barriers; however, it often times comes at a cost. I experienced "mommy guilt" for not always being mentally present for my children. Although I made an effort to attend every dance competition and sporting event, I would not be completely transparent if I said I was always engaged and enthusiastic. Not only was I exhausted from spending hours in school and completing assignments, but my program also required me to complete unpaid practicum hours (at least 20 hrs. a week) to help sharpen my clinical skills. Needless to say, rest was the only self-care I wanted.

In addition to managing mommy duties, I am a wife. Marriage is already challenging with learning to compromise, navigating finances, and unconditionally loving someone through difficult times. But, when a spouse decides to take on the task of obtaining a doctorate degree, their union is tested. Managing quality time and adjusting to financial instability becomes the new norm. As a result, my husband and I had to redefine roles and expectations as well as adopt patience and understanding. We honestly had to assess our marriage and decide whether the love we shared was strong enough to endure. Nonetheless, and five years later, my children are now 21, 16, 13, and 10 and are thriving (despite the many headaches I've endured from raising teenagers) and in spite of ups and downs, I am still married to my husband, now 17 years.

Upon reflecting on what motivated me to enter a doctoral program, I was primarily influenced by my upbringing, undergraduate/graduate coursework, and clinical practicum experiences. My experiences and academic curiosity led me toward a career path, in which I could understand individual and group dynamics by observing, assessing, and encouraging others during life's turbulent times.

While my journey toward helping others began at an early age, my professional training commenced as an undergraduate student. Throughout my academic career, I was drawn to learning more about the field of psychology and continued to gain knowledge and practical experiences, which eventually led me to completing a Bachelor's in psychology and obtaining three Master degrees in education, professional counseling, and clinical psychology. While working in the mental health field, I began to observe generational patterns of depression, anger, and trauma, which appeared to be pervasive in underserved communities. I felt ill-equipped to provide quality care and recognized the importance of returning to school in order to learn the necessary skills to be an effective mental health clinician. Additionally, I began feeling an urge to support Black women, as their needs have historically been overlooked in the face of supporting the needs of others. As a result of observing pervasive mental health conditions in underserved communities and a desire to support Black women, my professional goal is to open multiple private practices that seek to provide quality services to women using a holistic approach toward healing. In the end, I want to empower Black women and other women of color to emphatically proclaim, *I Am Not Who They Say I Am, I Am More!*

Professional Experiences

There is no surprise that society, the media, and socialization experiences influence how one is perceived when being both Black and a woman in America. Black women have been perceived as a pillar of strength within their community, in their family, and relentlessly the backbone of many socio-political movements. Historically, they have supported others even when their own needs have not been met. My experiences as a Black woman pursuing a doctorate has, at times, come with disrespect and unfair assumptions or have been relegated to stereotypical roles assigned to Black women like nurturing, obliging, and/or accommodating to White counterparts, especially in positions of power.

One memory I can share occurred during my third-year practicum experience. Typically, I consider myself to be quite the social butterfly in my personal life; however, at work, I willingly put on the hat of being focused, maintaining integrity, and always being professional. These characteristics might seem rudimentary, but as Black women, we tend to be hyper-vigilant about others' perceptions with the hope of dispelling misconceptions. All things considered, my supervisor, a White woman, and another mental health professional, also White, were engaged in a conversation about Halloween costumes. In my presence, they wrestled with the idea of wearing Blackface as part of a Halloween costume and questioned the sensitivity level of those who rejected the notion. At that moment, I never felt more invisible! How could two educated women invalidate the experiences of my people and more importantly, how do I address this hurtful experience with someone in a position of power without being perceived as angry, even though that is exactly how I felt. With the support and guidance of my program chair, who encouraged me to advocate for myself, I ended up having a meaningful conversation with my supervisor who profusely apologized for her ignorance. All in all that issue was resolved, but I couldn't help but be frustrated about why I am constantly in situations where I have had to censor my feelings or water down my reaction for the betterment of others.

Furthermore, I wondered how many other professional Black women have had the same experiences. It was because of my experiences and others alike that I chose a dissertation topic that would give voice to professional Black women by investigating their experiences while being enrolled in a doctoral program. The purpose of my study was to elucidate the needs of professional Black women, specifically those that identified as a Strong Black Woman (SBW) and inform academic institutions of ways to support this population. Results indicated that participants identified a myriad of positive attributes to describe themselves, had a strong desire to dispel misconceptions of Black women, and communicated a need for mentorship from other professional Black women.

Given the results of my dissertation, it appears that other Black women pursuing doctoral degrees have had similar experiences. Consequently, I now have a strong desire to support Black women both therapeutically and by means of mentorship. My hope is that those who are mentored will pay it forward to other matriculating doctoral students, ultimately cultivating a culture that states, *I Am Not Who They Say I Am, I Am More!*

Conclusion & Closing Thoughts

To all the fantastic Black women currently pursuing their doctoral degree or considering, go for it! The journey will not be easy and you may experience periodic failure; however, the reward is priceless. When I have had moments of distress, I remember there is approximately 2% of the U.S. population that have obtained a doctoral degree. In fact, the 2017 U.S. census reported a total of 4,096 doctoral degree conferrals; 162 were women of African descent. We are few in number but have always been a mighty force in the world. It is important to remember the strength, fearlessness, and tenacity of our ancestors and use it as a source of empowerment. My final proclamation is for all the "anomalies" to stand up and show the world, I Am Not Who They Say I Am, I Am More!

About Janeé Stevenson

Janeé Stevenson, *Psy.D. Candidate, Clinical Psychology - Chestnut Hill College*, has a wealth of experience working clinically with various populations (children, adolescents, and adults); however, her passion is working with emerging adults in the college counseling setting. Her clinical and research interests include adjustment and achievement of emerging adults, relationship issues, multicultural issues, particularly, the effects of racism and discrimination on marginalized groups. Her recently defended dissertation, A Phenomenological Study of What It Means to be a Strong Black Woman for African American Women Pursuing a Doctoral Degree, sought to elucidate the needs of this group and inform academic institutions of ways to support African American women as they pursue a terminal degree.

Janeé is a student-affiliate member of the American Psychological Association (APA), Pennsylvania Psychological Association (PPA), New Jersey Psychological Association (NJPA), and The Association of Black Psychologists (ABPsi).

Tiffany Brannon

"Work Smarter Not Harder"

Success is a Journey Not a Destination

By: **Tiffany Brannon, M.Ed, LPC, CSOTP Supervisee**

Introduction

Born and raised in Lexington, Kentucky I was blessed to have a great family including my mother, father and two younger brothers. My parents divorced when I was in elementary school as a result my mother raised me for a while independently. I was the first person on my mother's side of the family to attend college. I earned my Master's in Counseling in Professional Counseling from Lindsey Wilson College in Kentucky in 2011. I am currently a student in the University of Cumberlands Ph.D. program for Counseling, Education and Supervision with a focus in Leadership. I am a practicing mental health clinician in the state of Virginia where I have been for the past two years, however prior practiced in Kentucky for six years. As a therapist, I have the pleasure of assisting countless in different focus areas. I am honored to be a part of this project to share my experiences as a single mother on a professional journey.

Personal Experiences: Education is Important

As a child growing up without many resources, it was still my goal to "have the highest level of education possible" because as a child I figured out early on that education was important. I became pregnant with my oldest daughter when I was seventeen years old as a senior at Lafayette High School in Lexington, KY. Despite the circumstance, I still attempted to push forward. Taking honors classes throughout high school helped me to take on fifteen credit hours in community college enrolled as a pre-med student for Psychiatry. That changed, along with my major, when I had my second daughter. I pushed through community college, graduated and then enrolled at Eastern Kentucky University (EKU) in their Psychology program. The program was so difficult for me that I withdrew from several classes, failed several classes and retook many courses however I eventually graduated with a Bachelors in Arts of Psychology. As a single mother working full time and enrolled in school full time, it was very difficult. However, I did not let that get in my way. My daughters were my primary inspiration and source of motivation to keep pushing forward no matter how hard it became for me. At this point I thought, I made it! I can get a job however the job market required a Master's Degree. I was not prepared for this at all.

The Master's program at EKU had participants with high GPA's, accolades, community service and I had none of that. I knew I could not get in because I barely obtained my Bachelor's degree. Four years passed, during this time I worked for the Fayette County School system as a substitute teacher and teacher assistant. I heard about a Master's program that would work around your work schedule and had conditional enrollment. Of course, I needed someone to explain to me what conditional enrollment was and what I needed to do. I applied to the Masters in counseling program under "conditional enrollment". I was able to successfully pass all my courses the first semester earning a 3.45 GPA. That was the highest GPA I had ever received in my life. I was able to dedicate three weekends a month for two consecutive years to earn my Masters.

At this point, I worked full time as well resulting in a crazy schedule. As a single mother I would get off work at 2:30, drive to my daughters' school to pick them up, drop them off at the sitter and then attempt to be at class on time at 4:00 p.m. It was hard and unfortunately, I always received jokes and remarks that I was always "late" but I never let that bother me. As a single mother, it was literally up to me and only me to get it done. I could no longer rely on other people. This directly affected my social life as a result of having class four hours a night and eight hours on Saturdays, I was exhausted. I had just enough time to study and complete assignments on the weekend.

At times I would come home Friday from work on weekends I did not have class and did not leave my home until Monday morning when leaving for work. This caused me to become more distant with close friends and created a wedge, unfortunately. Like they say, "Anything in Life Worth Having Is Worth Working For". My oldest daughter at the time was diagnosed with brain cancer in 2009 and I am so blessed to have had the amount of support from my employer and the University during that time period.

Professional Experiences: Taking Another Direction

My daughter eventually became stable and coincidentally at the time a colleague and professor I knew from Lindsey Wilson was spearheading a doctoral program at the University of the Cumberlands (UC). The professor along with a group of other professors had the program ready to go. I applied, wrote essays, drove an hour to interview face to face, and took the entrance exam and was admitted in Spring 2013. I never in my life thought I could ever get into a doctoral program. My original plan was to evaluate programs to see if I could even get admission after my fortieth birthday (goals I envisioned). But I could not pass up this opportunity. I hit the ground running and was presented with so many opportunities that it was initially overwhelming. I joined a sorority, Zeta Phi Beta, Incorporated which was a blessing!

I was able to learn how to present at a conference by facilitating a breakout session, roundtable, and poster sessions. I had the privilege of becoming the President of the Counseling Honors Society, Chi Sigma Iota, at UC coordinating community service events and more! I had the opportunity to reactivate the Kentucky Counseling Association's (KCA) division for the Association of Multicultural Counseling and Development (AMCD) and acting President. I was also presented with an award as the 2015 Graduate Student of the Year for the Kentucky Counseling Association at their annual convention, where I had the opportunity to present three times at their state conference. Furthermore, I was presented with the opportunity to work with the national organization of AMCD and earned a research grant award.

All my dedication to my children and studies were my priority. I met my husband and we wed Fall 2016 relocating me to Virginia as a result in June 2016. Once in Virginia I was appointed the President of the Virginia Counseling Association's AMCD division the summer of 2016 and am currently on their Executive Board presently as Secretary. I also serve as the Social Media Chair and Co-Chair of the Professional Development Committee for the Virginia Counseling Association.

In Kentucky, I was consistently encouraged and supported by the clinical director/owner of the organization I worked for, Mr. Lee. Unfortunately, there is a negative stigma associated with working on your doctorate. Granted, I do not have a doctorate degree however it seems once people know you are working towards one it does affect their perception of you one way or another. Once moving to Virginia I did not realize that having my doctoral experience on my resume would affect job obtainment. In interviews, employers would directly ask me "Why are you here if you are working on a doctorate?" as if being in school equated to having a doctoral level job. As soon as I removed the doctoral portion from my resume', I began to receive job offers from every interview. This was shocking to me. As a result, I do not tell anyone I am working on my Ph.D., at all even to this day. Maybe this will change when I finish.

I, unfortunately, have had several riffs in my doctoral process. I changed my topic twice. I then moved forward with my committee of three, one black male professor, one white female professor and my chair was a white male. They encouraged me and provided me with much guidance and assistance. I began to make great progress until my chair suddenly left the University. At the time I was on maternity leave early 2018. That resulted in several professors resigning and as a result, I found out my chair could no longer be on my committee nonetheless be my dissertation chair. As a result, fortunately, I still have the same committee members but I do have a new chair however he has been very supportive, compassionate and reliable during this emotional change and transition. This change also resulted in my research focus changing from quantitative to qualitative.

Professionally I am currently a clinical supervisor. Prior to that, I worked at a residential facility in Virginia with treatment programs for youth in order to help them overcome behavioral health problems. The programs address comprehensive mental health needs and give residents the tools they need for a complete recovery in the following areas: self-injurious behaviors, suicidal behaviors, and intellectual disabilities, sexual abusive youth (offenders) programs for general and intellectual disabilities and assessment/diagnostic program.

Conclusion & Closing Thoughts

No matter what is going on in your life you have to ask yourself, "Is this my highest level of potential?" If not then assess and evaluate what obstacles and barriers are getting in your way. Sometimes it may seem like the world is against you. Push through. Also, remember to try to have a good balance in your life including fun and an active social life. Identify what your inner strength is and use that to push you through all adversity in your life. My most recent accomplishment has been giving birth to my awesome, happy and handsome son. I love him so much! In closing, I want to say that if I could do anything differently on my journey, it would be to "work smarter, not harder". Once you figure that out, it can be life changing.

About Tiffany Brannon

Tiffany Brannon is a native of Lexington, KY and is a current Ph.D. student in Counseling Education and Supervision at the University of the Cumberlands. She received her Bachelor's degree in Psychology with a concentration in Juvenile Justice from Eastern Kentucky University. Tiffany graduated with honors from Lindsey Wilson College with a Masters of Counseling in Education.

As a first-generation college student, Tiffany has advocated for youth and women in her hometown by creating and developing an annual youth leadership conference for middle & high school age girls. Furthermore, Tiffany has created and implemented a professional business network for Black Women in Kentucky that plans to become nationwide.

Tiffany's current research examines the Intersectionality of Adverse Childhood Experiences in Single Black Mothers. Tiffany has over five years of post-masters clinical experience and is currently a practicing clinician working with youth addressing significant mental health in a residential facility as a Certified Sex Offender Treatment Provider Supervisee in the state of Virginia. Tiffany also specializes in substance abuse, domestic violence (offenders and victims), trauma (sexual abuse/violence), anger management, generalized anxiety and other mental health diagnoses in youth and adult populations.

Tiffany is a wife and mother of three children. She is an active member of Zeta Phi Beta Sorority, Incorporated as well as the American Counseling Association. She has been active at the state level in the Kentucky Counseling Association on their Executive Board and currently sits on the Executive Board for the Virginia Counseling Association.

54265196R00063

Made in the USA
Columbia, SC
30 March 2019